MICHEL FOUCAULT

MICHEL FOUCAULT

AN INTRODUCTION

Philip Barker

Edinburgh University Press

© Philip Barker, 1998

Reprinted 2001, 2003

Transferred to Digital Print 2010

Edinburgh University Press
22 George Square, Edinburgh

Typeset in Caslon
by Pioneer Associates Ltd, Perthshire, and
Printed and bound in Great Britain by
CPI Antony Rowe, Chippenham and Eastbourne

A CIP record for this book is available from the
British Library

ISBN 0 7486 1038 3

This book is dedicated to the life of Robert 'Tyler' Miazek

[one of those]...who are impatient and gloomily inclined towards themselves and in all they do resemble rampaging horses, and who derive from their own works, indeed, only a shortlived fire and joy which almost bursts their veins and then a desolation and sourness made more wintry by the contrasts it presents – how should such men endure to remain within *themselves*! They long to dissolve into something *'outside'* . . .

Nietzsche, *Daybreak – Thoughts on the Prejudices of Morality*

Born 10 February 1953, committed suicide 2 November 1996

CONTENTS

ACKNOWLEDGEMENTS

I would like to thank the following people who in different ways assisted in the production of this work: Jan Barker, Yvette Blackwood, Rebecca Butterworth, Jackie Jones, David Lawton, Dan O'Neil, Christine Standish and Peter Thomas. Special thanks go to John Frow and Graeme Turner for allowing me to use the English Department at the University of Queensland as my intellectual home from the middle of 1995 to the end of 1997.

I have a long-standing intellectual debt to Stephen Knight, Elizabeth Grosz and John O. Ward.

COPYRIGHT PERMISSIONS

Part of Chapter 6, 'Thinking Against Foucault', was previously pub-
lished in a different form as 'Foucault's sublime: E-mail to Postumius
Terentianus', in *Foucault: The Legacy*. Edited by Claire O'Farrell,
Queensland University of Technology, Brisbane, 1997.

INTRODUCTION

The aim of this book is a modest one, to provide a number of entry points into the work of Michel Foucault in a way that is clear, is easy to read and avoids an overly technical vocabulary. Chapters 1 to 5 directly examine major features of Foucault's work. Chapters 6 and 7 are Foucauldian departures that illustrate some of the possibilities that are opened up by his work: Chapter 6 directs its attention to philosophical issues, and Chapter 7 to literary themes. The major Foucauldian themes taken up in each chapter are detailed in the Contents.

The issue of reading a text, and the function of commentary, is explored in Chapters 1 and 6. Chapter 5 examines *The Order of Things* and *The Archaeology of Knowledge* and covers some of Foucault's more demanding material. Although this book is structured so that each chapter is self-contained and therefore can be read in any order, it is suggested that readers with no prior knowledge of Foucault might find it easier to read Chapter 5 after Chapters 1 to 4.

In order to draw out the background for my reading of Foucault's work, I shall begin by briefly examining Foucault's attitude to the Enlightenment and the work of modernity which for the most part occurs in the paper 'What is Enlightenment?':[1]

> Enlightenment must be considered both as a process in which men participate collectively and as an act of courage to be accomplished personally. Men are at once elements and agents of a single process. They may be actors in the process to the extent that they participate in it; and the process occurs to the extent that men decide to be its voluntary actors.[2]

Foucault suggests that the important issue raised here by Kant is that 'men' are at once both elements and agents in the process of engaging in the task *Aude sapere*: 'dare to know', 'have the courage, the audacity, to know'[3] – to know, or come to an understanding of the conditions under which the Enlightenment can find a way out of a state of immaturity, which Foucault suggests should be thought of as an exemplary attitude for us in respect of 'modernity'.

> And by 'attitude', I mean a mode of relating to contemporary reality; a voluntary choice made by certain people; in the end, a way of thinking and feeling; a way, too, of acting and behaving that at one and the same time marks a relation of belonging and presents itself as a task. A bit, no doubt, like what the Greeks called an *ethos*. And consequently, rather than seeking to distinguish the 'modern era' from the 'premodern' or 'postmodern', I think it would be more useful to try to find out how the attitude of modernity, ever since its formation, has found itself struggling with attitudes of 'countermodernity'.[4]

Foucault argues that Kant's unique interrogation of the Enlightenment addresses two questions: what is the present today, which is framed by the difference that the present introduces in respect of yesterday?; and what is the possibility of fabricating an 'exit' or a 'way out'?[5] Foucault suggests that this attitude of modernity to the present is characterised by 'a consciousness of the discontinuity of time: a break with tradition, a feeling of novelty, of vertigo in the face of the passing moment'. However, what is most interesting about this encounter is that it offers us the possibility of transforming our relation with ourselves.

> To be modern is not to accept oneself as one is in the flux of the passing moments; it is to take oneself as the object of a complex and difficult elaboration: what Baudelaire, in the vocabulary of his day, calls *dandysme*.[6]

Foucault proposes that both the possibility of a 'transformational' attitude to oneself in the present and the constitution of oneself as an autonomous subject are rooted in the Enlightenment. The consequence of this is that whenever one takes up a position in the postmodern/countermodern debate today, one cannot escape the fact that it is our contemporary reception of the Enlightenment which marks out the possibilities of where one can stand, what one can say and so on. It is therefore not a question of being for or against the Enlightenment; rather, what should be undertaken is a series of enquiries that examine problematics derived from the Enlightenment, which in turn transform our relation with it and with ourselves.[7]

Perhaps this view can be extended a little further, and the suggestion made that care should also be taken to avoid being placed in a situation of being for or against postmodernism, or even for or against Foucault. Would it not be more productive to use those aspects of Foucault's work that are found to be useful and reject those that are not, while maintaining at all times a critical attitude towards it? For, if Foucault has achieved anything at all that is worthwhile, it is that his work is resistant to all dogmatisms, not only because it problematises certainties wherever it encounters them, but also because it problematises the conditions of its own existence. This is surely also the question of 'life' today, to ceaselessly and endlessly ask the question: what are the conditions and limits of our existence in the present?

My hope is that, together in the pages of this book, we will be able to leave the drab monotony of modernity behind us and explore Foucault's optimistic and colourful nominalist world, where one is able to delight in the pleasure of the journey and, in those fearful moments of sceptical doubt and anxiety, recall Foucault's thought that the object of intellectual activity is to 'think differently'. So, please read on . . . and just enjoy . . .

NOTES

1. M. Foucault, *The Foucault Reader*, ed. Paul Rabinow (New York: Pantheon Books, 1984): 'What is Enlightenment?', pp. 32–50.
2. Ibid., p. 35.
3. This has resonances with Foucault's critique of man as the impossible double in the social sciences, being both their subject and object. See Chapter 2 of this book, 'Power, Truth and Strategy', and Chapter 5, 'Thought from the Outside'.
4. Foucault, op. cit., *The Foucault Reader*, p. 39.
5. Ibid., p. 34.
6. Ibid., p. 41.
7. This should not be confused with the project of humanism, which involves the discovery or rediscovery of a set of themes or experiences of the universal subject. See Chapter 6, 'Thinking Against Foucault'.

1

—————— · ——————

BODY AND TEXT

It is difficult to know how to begin. How to find a position for myself which will enable the flow of discourse to run across the page, and allow me to write about so diverse and complex a figure as Foucault? Indeed, what kind of relation would it be possible to have with his work, that would be not reductive but sensibly expansive? This thought leaves me in a state of unsettled hesitation which I understand perfectly well, acknowledging that to present *my* Foucault in this book risks congealing that name and eliminating all those other Foucaults already in existence, and others yet to come.

However, perhaps putting the question of how my work can relate to Foucault without freezing other interpretations into a more typically Foucauldian formulation will allow a beginning to emerge: how is it possible to avoid the trap of commentary while at the same time engaging in a form of critical interaction that is productive, interesting and useful?

Before us lies a text – [this text] bound by its physical form which points to an originating moment in the hand of the author, a conjunction between hand and text, that draws us towards reading the text as a 'personal' puzzle, apparently endorsed by this originating moment. As if by chance, we might unexpectedly find ourselves speaking of the relation between the life of the author and the meaning of text, where the text becomes *nothing* but an index of this life, linked together by the sequence of moments when the hand was inscribing the characters on the page that we now see before us.[1]

In an extreme form, this style of 'biographical' criticism reduces the text to an event-text in the unfolding continuum of the life of the author. It is assumed that the author is in control of the text and expresses himself or herself through it. In response to this, in order to uncover the *meaning* of the text, one adopts the strategy of reducing its many possible interpretations to those meanings that coincide with the known events of the author's life. This is a style of criticism that seems so familiar that it is genuinely difficult to pose this 'biographical' strategy as the kernel of a problem. Yet the weight of this familiarity might induce us, at least provisionally, to draw out potential problems that pose questions for us.

To undertake this, we must first separate two things: the production of the text by its author, and the text in its materiality as it lies before us. We will then be in a position to ask two interrelated questions, at once so obvious and yet so difficult to formulate: What is an author? What is a text?[2] Foucault suggests that the categories of both author and text are unstable. Neither has always served the same function or acted in the same way throughout history. Moreover, it can be argued that the very conjunction between author and text is a modern phenomenon that is dependent on legal concepts such as copyright, the existence of a publishing system, the construction of disciplines such as 'literary' studies by universities and so on. However, if the conjunction author–text cannot provide us with transhistorical continuity, but rather is a recent historical event, then there is at least the possibility that the conjunction writer–text–death provides us with a more continuous relation.

Foucault argues that in early European culture one of the most important functions of storytelling was to provide immortality for an author by immortalising their name. In the Homeric tales and in Celtic myths, an often-repeated theme is that the hero will live forever through the continuing repetition of their name.[3] In this way, textual immortality is endowed on those who often die prematurely. A further recognition of the association between writing and death occurs in the story of the *One Thousand and One Arabian Nights*, where Scheherazade forestalls her death by telling stories from dusk until dawn and at the same time guarantees for herself a kind of immortality in the survival of her name.

In contrast to this, the disappearance of the author in our epoch inaugurates a separation between author and text, which allows the category of the author to be put into question. In certain forms of modernist writing, such as the work of James Joyce, the relation between writing and death has been reinvigorated and transformed, and the effect of a work such as *Ulysses* is precisely to disrupt the notion that an author is in control of the text.

This allows the author to be posed as a problem not to be resolved, in the sense of restoring the author to their place, but rather as a category to be analysed in terms of its functions and effects. Foucault suggests that the author is both more and less than a proper name, and offers the following example. If a particular person does not have certain specific physical attributes that we believe them to have, we would still assume that their proper name continues to refer to the same person that we had always known. Moreover, if we found out that they did not really live at a particular place, this would not alter the attachment of the name to the person to which it has always been attached. However, authors' names function quite differently.

It may be that if we learn that Shakespeare never lived in Stratford-on-Avon, it would not be a significant problem for the reader; however, if we learned that he never wrote any of the plays, but that they were written by Francis Bacon, the authors' names of both Shakespeare and Bacon would be considerably modified. Authors' names are not like proper names and do not relate to bodies in the same way that proper names do. What do they do, then?

Foucault argues that the name of an author acts as a system of classifying and organising a body of work. This functions in two ways: first, the author's name allows certain texts to be linked together; second, it gives a certain status to particular works within our culture:

> Its presence is functional in that it serves as a means of classification. A name can group together a number of texts. A name also establishes different forms of relationships among texts. Neither Hermes not Hippocrates existed in the sense that we can say Balzac existed, but the fact that a number of texts were attached to a single name implies that relationships of homogeneity, filiation, reciprocal explanation, authentication, or of common utilization were established among them. Finally, the author's name characterizes a particular manner of existence of discourse. Discourse that possesses an author's name is not to be immediately consumed and forgotten; neither is it accorded the momentary attention given to ordinary, fleeting words. Rather, its status and its manner of reception are regulated by the culture in which it circulates.[4]

The author's name operates as a function of discourse that is embedded in general cultural forms and that can be analysed. This analysis is indicative of the following: (1) Authors have become objects of appropriation, which is associated with the development of concepts of property, ownership and the copyright system. (2) The author function is not a universal, nor a constant in every form of discourse. For example, there have always been texts that do not require authors: folk tales, epics and so on. (3) The author function is not spontaneously located in individuals, it emerges from a range of operations which construct the 'rational' entity we call an author. (4) The author function is indicative of how one should critically relate to a text, insofar as:

(a) the author explains the presence of certain events within a text;
(b) the author constitutes a principle of unity in writing;
(c) the author neutralises contradictions that are found in a series of texts;
(d) the author is a unified form of expression covering the totality of their printed words.

(5) The author function is not just a simple reconstruction after the fact of the existence of a text, because texts do bear signs of the specific moment of their production, in terms of personal pronouns, adverbs of time and place and the conjunction of verbs. However, these stylistic connections do not constitute a set of meanings, and operate quite differently in texts with authors and texts without them.

Foucault summarises these five aspects of the author function in the following way:

> the 'author-function' is tied to the legal and institutional systems that circumscribe, determine, and articulate the realm of discourses; it does not operate in a uniform manner in all discourses, at all times, and in any given culture; it is not defined by the spontaneous attribution of a text to its creator, but through a series of precise and complex procedures; it does not refer, purely and simply, to an actual individual insofar as it simultaneously gives rise to a variety of egos and to a series of subjective positions that individuals of any class may come to occupy.[5]

In summary, Foucault's argument is that while to some extent writing has always been attributed to a proper name (such as Aristotle, Homer and so on), it is the conjunction of the development of the notion of the individual, the ownership of intellectual property and the copyright and publishing distribution regime that gives birth to the modern author.[6]

If Foucault's account of the emergence of the author and the author function is convincing, it has significant consequences for literary criticism. In particular, it raises the question: how is it possible to undertake the task of non-biographical, non-authorial criticism? There are many possible methodological responses to this question, including among others Formalism and Psychoanalysis. However, for Foucault each of these approaches has specific effects. Formalism assumes an endlessly repeated structure lying in wait to capture every possible interpretation and restore to it its relation to its true place/ meaning; while a psychoanalytic interpretation depends upon a transversal meaning-structure hanging over a text waiting to restore to it truth either as an interpretive effect, or by constructing a series of links between the psychoanalytic life of the author-subject and their work.

This is not to suggest that any of these or indeed any other interpretive technique may not provide for productive work, but following Foucault we might want to ask to what extent each critical methodology to which we appeal already expresses a relation to a pre-existing transhistorical subject, a pre-existing transhistorical structure or a universal element. This element, which precedes it and at the same time makes its appearance possible, disallows the possibility of either fabricating an account of the specific moment of the emergence of the modern subject or providing for an analysis of the work of that subject which takes this specific emergence into account. This returns us to the simultaneous emergence of the modern author and the modern text, and the possibility of trying to establish a critical inter-action that would allow one to analyse a particular text in its own terms, in the face of its specific material existence. Such a critical interaction would also have to acknowledge both the emergence and the disappearance of particular subjects in discourse.

This takes us back to the second of our opening questions: What is a text? Insofar as a text is a published work that is distributed within and perhaps between cultures, it is more than just writings on a page, it is a commodity in circulation. While all writing has the potential to become a text, how this occurs in a particular instance can be a complex procedure, and editors are well aware of the difficulty of creating a 'text'. The construction of Nietzsche's *Will to Power* from scattered fragments, some apparently even written on the back of laundry bills, serves as an illustration of how 'writing' is transformed during the collecting and editing process and takes on the status of 'text'.[7] However, there is already a further issue here that it might be worth considering.

As the text sits before us on the table, a series of questions can be posed (which emerge from our disqualifying, at least temporarily, the involvement of the author, in the light of our earlier discussion): What enabled this particular text to draw out the specific discourse that we find emerging from it? Why this particular discourse and no other? Why this particular set of statements from all those which could be presented? There are three dimensions of this to be discussed. First, the operation of the publishing and copyright systems. Second, what it is about a particular discourse that might lead it to be prevented from being circulated. Third, what it is that enables something to be counted as knowledge 'worthy' of circulation in the culture.[8]

Foucault suggests that in every society there are mechanisms for distributing, regulating and controlling the circulation of texts. In Western culture, two of the most prominent ones are *exclusion* and *prohibition*. We are all well aware that in any given situation there are things that cannot be said, which suggests to Foucault the existence of mechanisms of prohibition. There are three types of prohibitions: those that deal with particular objects; those that are involved with ritual and all that surrounds it; and those that confer the exclusive right to speak about a particular subject. These reinforce each other and operate to form a web of prohibitions constantly subject to modification.[9]

There is also another kind of exclusion that relates to the principle of division and rejection and is constituted around the opposition reason/folly.[10] This opposition locates madness in the meaninglessness of the speech of the mad, even if at times beyond this meaningless dialogue it is assumed that there lies a secret reason, all the more rational because it originates from under the surface of meaningless babble. This is the basis on which psychoanalysts and psychiatrists listen attentively to the speech of the mad only to reinforce in the speaker the knowledge that they must understand that their mad speech represents something unknown to them, to which only the analyst or psychiatrist can lead them.[11]

The final series of exclusions operates around the distinction between true and false and emerges against the background of how it is that certain statements or propositions are taken to be true while others are taken to be false. Foucault describes this as the 'will to truth' which relies on institutional support and is part of a more general deployment of the will to knowledge in Western society:

> it is both reinforced and accompanied by whole strata of practices such as pedagogy – naturally – the book system, publishing, libraries, such as the learned societies in the past, and laboratories today. But it is probably even more profoundly accompanied by

the manner in which knowledge is employed in a society, the way in which it is exploited, divided and in some ways attributed.

... I have spoken at greatest length about the third. With good reason: for centuries the former [prohibited words and the division of madness] have continually tended toward the latter [the will to truth]; because this last has, gradually, been attempted to assimilate the others in order to both modify them and to provide them with a firm foundation. Because, if the two former are continually growing more fragile and less certain to the extent that they are now invaded by the will to truth, the latter in contrast, daily grows in strength, in depth and implacability.[12]

The educational system validates certain discourses insofar as it 'is a political means of maintaining or of modifying the appropriation of discourse, with the knowledge and the power it carries with it'.[13] It is itself part of the ritualisation of the world, which qualifies certain people to speak about certain subjects in the form of a discourse which in turn founds the *subject* of discourse. This marks the beginning of a double play as the author becomes the founding or grounding instance of a particular form of the subject. The *subject* and the author fold into each other as a consequence of the distribution, circulation and validation of certain discourses which privileges particular modes of relating to the world. In this way, the *subject* emerges out of the possibilities of discourse as a mode of relating to oneself as both a subject and an object of discourse.

If the example of psychoanalysis is considered in this light, it is clear that there are people in the world in whom the construction of the relation 'between themselves' is mediated by psychoanalytic theory. Psychoanalysis as a discursive formation enables the possibility of psychoanalytic subject positions – castrated, narcissistic, Oedipal and so on. This is independent of whether we might want to refer to 'psychoanalysis' as a theory that represents a 'True' account of the world. Indeed, both psychoanalysis and the theory of the independent, self-sustaining subject (*cogito*) presuppose a founding experience of the subject that in the case of psychoanalysis can be restored to it, or in the case of the self-sustaining subject is already known to itself.

In contrast to this, Foucault asks that the possibility be considered that the subject emerges from within discourse and is not in control of it in the everyday sense that we might understand.[14] It is his view that the subject emerges from the tendency of language to disrupt, fragment and shatter, and it is as a consequence of this that the author arrives, in the face of the danger of discourse, both as the point of its coherence and also as that which provides the index of responsibility for the possible meaning(s) of the text.

This is a difficult issue to come to terms with. What does it mean to say that the possibilities of the fundamental relation which we have with ourselves are already to some extent determined by the formation of discourse in which we find ourselves? Does this not seriously undermine the commonsense feeling we have of ourselves as experiencing a continuity of 'humanity' that stretches back through the Renaissance, to the Romans, the Greeks and even perhaps to the dawn of time?

When we look at prehistoric cave paintings, do we not consider that these marks and traces on the wall before us represent a fundamental relation that the painter has with him or herself and that we can experience in ourselves again today? We may be aware that we cannot see the same animals which have long since become extinct, but we are sure that we can experience the 'same' feelings of love, joy, pleasure, fear, freedom and so on. We are confident that what binds these experiences together is a point of stability and coherence, in the fashion of an author/subject, that is common to every experience of what it is to be human.

It is precisely this commonsense view that Foucault calls into question, suggesting that discourse is a specific historical event that incorporates its own series of possibilities and is bordered by *discontinuity*. We should therefore think of a particular discourse, not in terms of the expression of the universal themes of the author or subject, but rather as an event opened up by a specific culture at a particular moment – an event and an opening from which the subject/author emerges, in the face of an emergence that is only possible insofar as one is able to break up the conserving continuum of the past. This leads to the possibility that both the subject and history draw *discontinuity* into their very fabric.

If we imagine the past as a continuous series of events, we are able to ask the question of how this series can be broken up into segments that it will be possible to analyse historically. Typically, we do this by dividing the timeline into historical epochs or themes, for example the *French Revolution*, the *First Empire* and so on. Yet these divisions that seem at once so natural and obvious are already the effect of a number of choices that have been made in respect of how the object of historical research is constituted. For every continuity there is also a rupture, break or *discontinuity*. There is no particular reason why we could not constitute as the object of our historical study, Southern France 1725–88; however, to do so would be to decentre the significance of the French Revolution and the year 1789 and introduce a *discontinuity* into the way we have habitually thought about this particular epoch.

Discontinuity also comes into play at another level as it attempts to address the issue of how it is that a social formation ceases to 'think as it has been thinking up till then and begins to think other things in a new way'.[15] If we want to strategically abandon ideas of progress and development as we undertake our analysis, then attempting to come to terms with the difference between Renaissance thought and the Classical thought of the seventeenth century requires the introduction of a radical *discontinuity* between the two systems of thought.

> Ultimately, the problem that presents itself is that of the relations between thought and culture: how is it that thought has a place in the space of the world, that it has its origin there, and that it never ceases, in this place or that to begin anew?[16]

There is a further complication to be brought into this. There is no doubt that a relation exists between progress, development, the security of continuous history and the continuity or continuum of the author/subject.[17] This takes us back to the beginning of this chapter. If the category of the author is a principle of classification that serves to provide the ground against which concepts of subjectivity emerge and take their particular form, and if the discourse against which they emerge has a relation to the way that it circulates against the background of a regime of truth, the copyright and publishing systems, educational institutions and so on, this surely disqualifies the ways in which we usually undertake textual criticism – and in particular the very dense relation between textual criticism and commentary.

It is a consequence of Foucault's position that some of the particular difficulties of commentary be recognised. Commentary always presupposes something more than the text in front of one, a remainder or an excess of meaning that awaits discovery. It also imagines that in the course of time, as the density of the commentary increases, the text will finally be reduced to *its* meaning, a meaning that will be fixed and perhaps immutable. In this sense, commentary functions to attempt to reduce the text to a singular identity with itself, which in turn becomes part of the reductive strategy of the history of Western metaphysics.[18]

What are the implications of the main features of the analysis that has just been presented? First, it does not imply that we can never use an author's name again, but rather that we should recognise that if we undertake an exclusively psychological or biographical account of a text we are 'effecting' the emergence of a particular account of the author, and by implication the subject and 'world'. Moreover, we must be aware that the text is an event within the circulation of discourse in culture, and that it can be treated not only in terms of what differentiates it from other texts circulating at the same time, but also in terms of what permits a certain set of statements to emerge. This is possible because the material existence of the writer is a cultural event in its own terms, and at a more general level is due to the particular operation of the rules of discourse.[19]

The style of textual criticism possible in the light of Foucault's account of the production of both author and text would look towards framing questions along the lines of the following:

> under what conditions and through what form can an entity like the subject appear in the order of discourse; what position does it occupy; what functions does it exhibit: and what rules does it follow in each type of discourse? In short, the subject (and its substitutes) must be stripped of its creative role and analysed as a complex and variable function of discourse.
> . . . New questions will be heard:
> 'What are the modes of existence of this discourse?'
> 'Where does it come from; how is it circulated; who controls it?'
> 'What placements are determined for possible subjects?'
> 'Who can fulfil these diverse functions of the subject?'
> Behind all these questions we would hear little more than the murmur of indifference:
> 'What matter who's speaking?'[20]

These are the questions that inform Foucault's analysis of the work of others, be it Roussel, Kant or Deleuze. It is not that the proper name is absent but rather that it functions only as a category against which to frame the analysis. For example, in his analysis of the work of Raymond Roussel, Foucault is interested not in how Roussel's work relates to his psychology but rather in what way the work creates an opening from which the possibility of Roussel as a subject emerges.[21]

It is precisely the disjunction between words, and things in the sense of the 'real', that language requires in order to come into existence and in turn bring about the emergence of the subject that unfolds through language. If language and the world were identical, language would be redundant; it would in fact *be* the world. Roussel speaks from within a fracture in language, from the space of the impossibility of language representing the world in its entirety. It is that same fracture that at the beginning of this chapter led to posing the question of how it would be possible to capture such a diverse thinker as Foucault within the pages of this little book – a Foucault who is tied to his work not by his psychology, but by his emergence from within the possibilities opened up by discourse in this epoch.

This relates closely to Foucault's uncommon view which, for want of a better description, we can term *materialist nominalism*. By this, it is meant that on the one hand Foucault denies the possibility of an intrinsic substantive connection between language and the world, but at the same time he insists that words are not just wind, that discourse is material and has effects in the world, indeed that the world is laced with and by discourse. As a consequence of this, at the one time Foucault can claim that he is a nominalist, and yet still acknowledge that the materiality of discourse creates the conditions for what it is possible to say and the limits of what it is to be at any given time.

> Well, it is the interest I have in modes of discourse, that is to say, not so much the linguistic structure which makes such a series of utterances possible, but rather the fact that we live a world in which things have been said. These spoken words in reality are not, as people tend to think, a wind that passes without leaving a trace, but in fact, diverse as are the traces they do remain. We live in a world completely marked by, all laced with, discourse, that is to say, utterances which have been spoken, of things said, of affirmations, interrogations, of discourses which have already occurred. To that extent, the historical world in which we live cannot be dissociated from all the elements of discourse which have inhabited this world and continue to live in it as the economic process, the demographic, etcetera, etcetera. Thus spoken language, as a language that is already present, in one way or another determines what can be said afterward either independent of or within the general framework of language.[22]

Words are both nominal and material. They do not relate to the world in a substantive way but they do have effects which include the way that we as *subjects* elaborate a relation to ourselves with the world.[23] However, from Foucault's point of view it is important not to assume that we are in control of these effects, or can predict what they might be, because it is from within the disjunction between words/language and the real that both ourselves and meaning emerge in an unpredictable way.[24]

Foucault's accounts of the subject, author, text and his nominalism have particular consequences for literary criticism.

(1) They suggest the value of an approach that would try to avoid establishing a biographical relation between the author and the text as foundational. This is not to suggest that 'some' biographical informa-tion may not be useful, but that one must remember that imagining that the meaning of the text is to be found in the 'intentionality' of the writer has consequences. In particular, it might lead to employing an interpretive strategy based on the assumption that if you know what the writer meant to do, then you know what the text means. This view involves a number of difficulties: first, it assumes that writers in particular, and subjects in general, do actually know why they do things. This is questionable in terms of a number of different theoretical paradigms. Second, in order to be able to pursue the intentional interpretive strategy, an assumption is made that there is an absolute division between author and text. This division becomes an irreducible space that first allows the separation between author and text, and then in a second movement emphasises the role of the author as active and in control of a text which is seen to be a blank page passively waiting to be filled.

This gives weight to the idea of the creative genius of the individual in command of discourse which is an expression of their creativity. However, is the initial moment of separation between creative genius and text as plausible as it intuitively seems? Do we not experience ourselves as a somewhat muddled-up relation of being between many things? Indeed, the fabrication of the creative genius can be seen as an attempt to put a frozen order on this flowing 'between' that we can experience as the condition of our existence.[25]

The intentional author or creative genius serves as an exemplary fantasy of how we imagine we would like to be: in control of our destiny, in charge of our fate and always operating in a world driven by what we intend, and the (improbable) likelihood that our ends and intentions will match. As an alternative, one could argue that the subject (by that I mean the relation we have with ourselves) is constructed and emerges out of the subject positions opened up by the possibilities of discourse in any epoch. Therefore, text and writer exist in a strange kind of symbiosis, in a movement of being between. Neither has any particular claim to precedence over the other, and so claims that privilege either writer or text can be analysed in terms of the effects that such claims induce.

(2) One might also want to avoid trying to establish the definitive meaning of the text. As has already been noted, language in the fundament of its very existence is unable to match exactly with the world. The 'Real', whatever it might be, must always escape total entrapment by language. To imagine that language can capture whatever *is* is to enter into the realm of theology and imagine that one has the power of the Word of god(s), where to say what is, is to bring *it* into existence. This is the dream of a Universal language that we all share and understand in the same way, a dream that because it connects words with the substance of things is paradoxically both material and metaphysical at the same time. It is material because it founds a fundamental relation between word and material substance, it is metaphysical because the possibility of guaranteeing this relation already presupposes a theology (or ontology).

The reductive search for *the* meaning of a text attempts to re-establish a moment of unity between word and object and in this sense invokes the origin, that time before the Fall when in an ecstatic Garden of Eden speech, meaning and materiality were one.[26] What things meant was what they meant. In addition to this, the search for meaning implies just that, a looking for something beyond the surface of the text that exists in excess of what is before us, that little bit more about which we must speak and interpret. Once again, we might want to ask: what is the effect of the search to establish a secure meaning?

(3) We might want to avoid basing our criticism on the history of traditions. We involve ourselves in the history of traditions when we separate one text from another in terms of a continuous historical aesthetics or thematics. This places our appreciation of a text in a continuum measured in terms of similarities and differences that are determined in advance insofar as they are part of an ongoing history of literature. This history has its peaks and troughs, its progress and its reverses, and is a history that is expected to be grasped and understood in its entirety.[27]

A Foucauldian style of textual criticism would analyse a text with the following questions in mind: what are its effects; why this collection of statements and not others; what subject positions does it open up; what political interests does it serve; what role does it play in the politics of truth; what specific speakers' benefit can be attributed to it; what are its modes of existence, distribution and circulation? These features can be grouped together under two general headings: the Emergence of the Statement and the Politics of Discourse.

THE EMERGENCE OF THE STATEMENT

The analysis of the Emergence of the Statement arises from posing the following question: why this statement and no other?, where a statement is defined as a particular discursive event from within the various possibilities opened up and shaped by a discursive formation.[28]

> What counts in the things said by men is not so much what they may have thought or the extent to which these things represent their thoughts, as that which systematises them from the outset, thus making them thereafter endlessly accessible to new discourses and open to the task of transforming them.[29]

This shaping takes the form of a systematisation which makes it possible for a statement to find its recognition in a discursive formation. Systematisation and validation operate to produce the possibility of particular statements in terms of an operation that acts in an unknown way on the producers of particular statements.[30]

The issue to be considered here is the rules of a discursive formation which must be followed in order that a particular statement that emerges from within it may find its home there. In Foucault's work, this is initially analysed in relation to those discourses that have something of the form of 'scientific' discourses, such as: naturalistic, economic or grammatical discourses in *The Order of Things*; medical discourse in *The Birth of the Clinic*; and psychiatry in *Madness and Civilisation*. In each of these cases, the objective is to intervene in the received and assumed history that each of these sciences has of their own emergence.

The project of *The Order of Things* and *The Birth of the Clinic* is not simply to undertake an analysis of the inside of language, of language in itself, but to demonstrate possible subject positions that are opened up by the emergence of the statement within a discursive field.

> The positions of the subject are also defined by the situation that it is possible for him to occupy in relation to the various

domains or groups of objects: according to a certain grid of explicit or implicit interrogations, he is the questioning subject and, according to a certain programme of information, he is the listening subject; according to a table of characteristic features, he is the seeing subject, and, according to a descriptive type, the observing subject; he is situated at an optimal perceptual distance whose boundaries delimit the weight of relevant information; he uses instrumental intermediaries that modify the scale of the information, shift the subject in relation to the average or immediate perceptual level, ensure his movement from a superficial to a deep level, make him circulate in the interior space of the body – from manifest symptoms to the organs, from the organs to the tissues, and finally from the tissues to the cells.[31]

There are always multiple subject positions, and different positions carry with them their own politics and political investments, which takes us on to the next of our two methodological strategies, *the politics of discourse*.

THE POLITICS OF DISCOURSE

The *politics of discourse* examines discourse in terms of what political interest it serves, how it participates in the politics of truth, what the speaker's benefit is, who speaks on behalf of whom and what particular subject positions emerge from it. This extends the text into the wider discursive field in terms of its effects rather than its internal organisation. There are two particularly interesting examples of this in Foucault's work: *Herculine Barbin* and *I, Pierre Rivière*.[32]

Herculine is a hermaphrodite who lived her life as a woman, and then came into contact with medical discourse which fabricated her legal identity as a man. Herculine's story is important because her physiology suggested a state of indeterminacy, of being between sexes or being both sexes. This materially challenged the possibility of establishing a singular 'true' sex, and created an opening where in a situation of indeterminacy the subject, rather than the medical profession, might elaborate themself in terms of an assumed sexuality.

This is not just a question of a subjective choice that would support an extreme psychological interpretation of Herculine; on the contrary, for the major part of her life Herculine *knows* she is a woman. It is not until the intervention of medical discourse into her life, as a result of a medical condition, that the question of her genital ambiguity *needs* to be resolved amid the intersection of medical and moral discourse.

The moral question involves Herculine's relationship (as a woman) with a female lover; the medical question is that of a newly emerging rejection of the sexual doubling of the hermaphrodite. These constellations of discourse become involved in a moral, juridico-legal determination that leads to the pronouncement that Herculine is, and always was, a man. The truth of Herculine's sex becomes the index of a true identity, an identity of the one, of the same. It is because of this that Herculine's clitoris *becomes* Abel's penis and the possibility of multiple genital arrangement becomes the single, the same, the masculine – the true. A 'truth' which is located at the deepest, most hidden core of what it is to be human: 'we now know that it is sex itself which hides the most secret parts of the individual: the structure of his fantasies, the roots of his ego, the forms of his relationship to reality. At the bottom of sex there is truth.'[33]

An epistemological and a moral imperative intersect against the background of the politics of discourse. The medical and legal dossier which accompanies the book and the lack of 'commentary' by the contributors to the volume serve to emphasise the way in which Herculine's story operates within an emerging politics of discourse and will to truth.

Where do we find the speaker's benefit in this? In this particular instance, in the emerging medical and legal regimes which are both concerned to establish themselves on the foundation of speaking 'true'. For the medical establishment, the case of Herculine is part of that need on the one hand to decipher a single true sex and on the other, and this is possible only in the light of the first, to establish the deviations, perversions and so on that are founded on the possibility of a true sex. This is necessary because the notion of deviation always presupposes an already existing question – deviation from what? To deviate from the norm – the true. It is the conjunction of medicine and morality that comes into play and which can be analysed in terms of *the politics of discourse*.

I, Pierre Rivière operates in a similar way. The text assembled by Foucault contains Pierre Rivière's writings bound along with the legal, medical and other documents relating to the case. These discourses, while referring to the same event – Rivière's crime – do not form a 'composite work nor an exemplary text', but rather a 'strange contest, a confrontation, a power relation, a battle among discourses and through discourses'.[34] This battle involves a number of different zones and combatants: the legal profession, the medical profession, the judiciary, the police, the newspapers and of course Rivière himself. Rivière's crime, text and their relation circulate unevenly among the discourses that spring up around them, changing the status and function of both text and perceptions of Rivière himself. Initially, Rivière's text is used to show that he is not mad and then later it is used to show that he is mad. In between these two events, the constellation of discourse surrounding Rivière and his text is modified and transformed. In the light of this, Foucault refuses to interpret Rivière's text

> because it was what we used as the zero benchmark to gauge the distance between the other discourses and the relations arising among them. Secondly, because we could hardly speak of it without involving it in one of the discourses (medical, legal, psychological, criminological) which we wished to use as our starting point in talking about it. If we had done so, we should have brought it within the power relation whose reductive effect we wished to show, as we ourselves should have fallen into the trap it set.[35]

To interpret Rivière's text would be to bring back into play those scientific discourses that established their foundational interpretive ground against texts and lives such as Rivière's. In other words, what would be involved would be the continuing fabricating of an ever-intensifying circular loop that entraps all those who enter into it. This text would become an expression of the psychology, medical condition and criminological intent of Rivière linking him to the murder as he becomes the author of both text and murder. This is why Foucault suggests that this authorial connection has the same problems as those that were mentioned previously in this chapter.

The text does not relate directly to the murders but rather is part of a whole complex 'web of relations woven between one and the other'.[36] Text and deed exist amid 'ever-changing relations', while interpretations of Rivière's text and life allow the emergence and consolidation of certain kinds of discourse, and produce an increasingly intense series of relations between them, allowing each to reinforce the other. The more that Rivière and his text are popularised and circularised, the more opportunities for the displaying of interpretive expertise appear.

> In short his deed/text was subjected to a threefold question of truth: truth of fact, truth of opinion, and truth of science. To a discursive act, a discourse in act, profoundly committed to the

rules of popular knowledge there was applied a question derived elsewhere and administered by others.[37]

In applying these questions and administering them, the *politics of discourse* came into play allowing, if not demanding, that representatives of these emerging disciplines speak their expertise, their 'science', and galvanise for themselves an authoritative place.

Foucault's critique of the author and the function of commentary and his analysis of discourse opens up the possibility of a novel kind of literary criticism. It does not stand above other approaches but rather takes the form of a specific methodology with specific effects. The value of it should be measured not in terms of engendering proximity to the 'true' text but rather in terms of the way in which its effects circulate, are distributed and engage with *the emergence of the statement* and *the politics of discourse*.

NOTES

1. See J. Miller, *The Passion of Michel Foucault* (New York: Simon and Schuster, 1993) for an example of this style of biographical criticism.
2. Michel Foucault, *Language, Counter-Memory, Practice* (New York: Cornell University Press, 1977), 'What Is an Author?', pp. 113–38.
3. See *The Iliad, Taín Bo Cualigne* and the *Mabinogion*.
4. Foucault, op. cit., p. 123.
5. Ibid., pp. 130–1.
6. Ibid., pp. 131–6 for Foucault's account of the initiators of 'discursive practices'.
7. Foucault, *The Archaeology of Knowledge*, trans. A. M. Sheridan Smith (London: Tavistock, 1972), p. 24.
8. What follows here is Foucault's negative account of power; for his 'positive' theory, see Chapters 2 and 3.
9. Foucault, *The Discourse on Language*, appendix to *The Archaeology of Knowledge*, trans. A. M. Sheridan Smith (New York: Pantheon Books, 1972), p. 216.
10. See Foucault, *Madness and Civilisation*, trans. Richard Howard (London: Tavistock, 1979).
11. Foucault, op. cit., *Discourse on Language*, pp. 216–17.
12. Ibid., p. 219.
13. Ibid., p. 227.
14. Ibid., pp. 227–8.
15. Foucault, *The Order of Things* (London: Tavistock, 1980), p. 50.
16. Ibid., p. 50.
17. See Chapter 4 for a discussion of this in detail.
18. For more on this, see Chapter 2.
19. These issues are discussed further in Chapters 3 and 5.
20. Foucault, op. cit., *Language, Counter-Memory, Practice*, pp. 137–8.
21. Foucault, *Death and Labyrinth: The World of Raymond Roussel*, trans. Charles Ruas (New York: Doubleday, 1986), pp. 164–5.
22. Ibid., p. 177.

23. See Chapter 3 for an examination of the other kinds of material practices that produce subjects.

24. G. Burchell, C. Gordon and P. Miller, *The Foucault Effect: Studies in Governmentality* (Hemel Hempstead: Harvester Wheatsheaf, 1991), M. Foucault, 'Questions of Method', p. 86: 'I would just like to find out what effects the question produces within historical knowledge. Paul Veyne saw this very clearly: it's a matter of the effect on historical knowledge of a nominalist critique itself arrived at by way of a historical analysis.'

25. For more on being *between*, see Chapter 7.

26. For more on this, see Chapter 2.

27. For more on Foucault's account of history, see Chapter 2.

28. This relates closely to Foucault's account of the *episteme* which is discussed in detail in Chapter 5.

29. Foucault, *The Birth of the Clinic*, trans. A. M. Sheridan (London: Tavistock, 1976), p. xix.

30. Foucault, op. cit., *The Order of Things*, p. xi.

31. Foucault, op. cit., *The Archaeology of Knowledge*, p. 52.

32. Foucault, *Herculine Barbin, Being the Recently Discovered Memoirs of a Nineteenth Century French Hermaphrodite*, trans. Richard McDougall (New York: Pantheon Books, 1980). Foucault, *I, Pierre Rivière, having slaughtered my mother, my sister, and my brother...* (Harmondsworth: Penguin Books, 1978). *Madness and Civilisation* can also be read in a similar way; see Foucault, op. cit., *Madness and Civilisation*.

33. Ibid., p. x.

34. Foucault, op. cit., *I, Pierre Rivière*, p. x.

35. Ibid., p. xiii.

36. Ibid., p. 201.

37. Ibid., p. 210.

2

POWER, TRUTH AND STRATEGY [1]

Two of the most controversial aspects of Foucault's work are his concept of power and its relation to the will to knowledge/truth. Both are underpinned by a critique of contemporary historiography and an attempt to redefine it.

> The history which bears and determines us has the form of a war rather than that of a language: relations of power, not relations of meaning. History has no 'meaning', though this is not to say that it is absurd or incoherent. On the contrary, it is intelligible and should be susceptible of analysis down to the smallest detail – but this in accordance with the intelligibility of struggles, of strategies and tactics. [2]

In the article 'Nietzsche, Genealogy and History', Foucault draws his argument out, suggesting that conventional historiography is involved with the search for the origin. This incorporates three postulates: (1) it is an attempt to capture the essence of things in the form of primordial truth; (2) it assumes that things are most precious at the moment of their birth; (3) the origin is the site of truth. [3] The origin presupposes an idyllic time before the Fall when the world, god and humanity existed in a timeless Platonic zone where Word and existence were one. [4] The present acts as a rupture from this and provides a distance from this moment which 'history' attempts to bridge. As a result of this, the reference to the origin founds the present on a metaphysics of loss from the past, and simultaneously introjects both that loss, and the possibility of its recovery, into the present, as a consequence of the application of a particular historical methodology.

Following Nietzsche, Foucault suggests that this relation to the 'origin' can be strategically broken down into two terms: *Entstehung* and *Herkunft*, which are translated as *descent* and *emergence*. *Descent* becomes a movement away from the search for the origin, to one which separates, fragments and traces differences even in the body of the individual. It 'seeks the subtle, singular, and subindividual marks that might possibly intersect in them (the individual) to form a network that is difficult to unravel'.[5] This view suggests that the body is not an inert substantial material, but is plastic and susceptible to change and alteration.[6]

Genealogical analysis locates itself within the articulation of the body and history and reveals a body laced by history and transformed by it, a body where for every particular form that appears others are obscured, in a process that is not progressive but proceeds without definitive end. As one form of the body is replaced by another, specific forms of subjugation are replaced by others and not by the end of all subjugation. *Descent* identifies accidents, deviations, diversions, errors and false appraisals. It attempts to discover that 'truth or being do not lie at the root of what we know and what we are, but the exteriority of accidents'.[7] In emphasising the connection between the body and *descent*, genealogy 'seeks to re-establish the various systems of subjection: not the anticipatory power of meaning but the hazardous play of dominations'.[8]

In contrast to this, *emergence* describes a particular moment of arising, amid a series of episodic relations that are part of any system of subjugation. The analysis of *emergence* separates out struggles between forces that constitute moments of *emergence* which are not the result of the will of the individual, who is the result of the interaction of forces. In this way, *emergence* is the designation of a space, a site where the struggle of forces takes place, a place of differentiation, an arena where struggles for domination which have no 'progressive' aim are realised within the play of dominations. No-one is in control, but nonetheless from it analysable effects emerge.[9]

> Humanity does not gradually progress from combat to combat until it arrives at universal reciprocity, where the rule of law finally replaces warfare; humanity installs each of its violences in a system of rules and thus proceeds from domination to domination.[10]

The process of interpretation seeking the meaning of the origin is already the effect of *emergence*, of the play of domination. If we consider this in respect of the history of morality, we can see that such a history is not one of the ever-increasing refining of moral issues. *Emergence* adopts the perspective that the desire for morality, for a set of rules of conduct, already presupposes a series of dominations the outcome of which is to prescribe: (1) that a shared set of values is necessary for the success of communal life; (2) that any particular set of values have emerged only because of their relation to struggles for domination.

The recognition of *descent* and *emergence* in genealogical analysis serves to intervene in traditional historiography and resist any attempt to employ a supra-historical methodology where 'the historian's history finds its support outside time and pretends to base its judgements on an apocalyptic objectivity'.[11] In contrast to this, genealogy is marked by its embodiment in the time of the moment: 'Genealogy means that I conduct the analysis on the basis of a present question'.[12] It is in this context that what emerges is dissociation, that is, the possibility of shattering 'the unity of man's being'.

> One has to dispense with the constituent subject, to get rid of the subject itself, that's to say, to arrive at an analysis which can account for the constitution of the subject within a historical framework. And this is what I would call genealogy, that is, a form of history which can account for the constitution of knowledges, discourses, domains of objects etc., without having to make reference to a subject which is either transcendental in relation to the field of events or ruins in its empty sameness throughout the course of history.[13]

The effect of a continuous historical methodology is precisely to return to us the belief that 'everything' can be understood in the past, a belief which is foundational in how 'man' constructs a secure relation of understanding to 'himself'. Non-genealogical history constructs those continuities on which is founded the continuity of what it is to be human. It neutralises, universalises and in a sense de-historicises precisely that which is most manufactured, constructed and elaborated in the present.

> We believe in the dull constancy of instinctual life and imagine that it continues to exert its force indiscriminately in the present as it did in the past . . . We believe, in any event, that the body obeys the exclusive laws of physiology and that it escapes the influence of history, but this too is false.[14]

How we elaborate ourselves as subjects, how our body feels to us, how we resist and collude in the play of dominations of our own materiality, are all called into question by the genealogical method. It is precisely those aspects of our existence that seem closest to us, that seem the most obvious, the most certain, the most profound – that give us the deepest, most secure understanding of what we are – that become the object of genealogical history. In this way, genealogical, effective history undermines the concept that traditional history, even if it is directed at what seems to be most stable and secure about ourselves, gives us a grounding on which to base other certainties:

> 'Effective' history differs from traditional history in being without constants. Nothing in man – not even his body – is sufficiently stable to serve as the basis for self-recognition or for understanding other men. The traditional devices for constructing a comprehensive view of history and for retracing the past as a patient and continuous development must be systematically dismantled. Necessarily, we must dismiss those tendencies that encourage the consoling play of recognitions. Knowledge, even under the banner of history, does not depend on 'rediscovery', and it emphatically excludes the 'rediscovery of ourselves'. History becomes 'effective' to the degree that it introduces discontinuity into our very being – as it divides our emotions, dramatizes our instincts, multiplies our body and sets it against itself. 'Effective' history deprives the self of the reassuring stability of life and nature, and it will not permit itself to be transported by a voiceless obstinacy toward a millennial ending. It will uproot its traditional foundations and relentlessly disrupt its pretended continuity. This is because knowledge is not made for understanding; it is made for cutting.[15]

'Effective' history necessarily incorporates the historian's own lines of descent. Traditional historians are always involved in the presentation of a perspective which masks the adoption of a methodology that presents itself as objective, and thus able to capture the real of the past. It is as if they imagine themselves to be the passive receptacle of history as a process that just reveals itself to them. Nothing could be further from the actual practice of the historian who in fabricating objective history creates a subject–object split in themselves, which confirms their own sense of subjectivity precisely at the moment when they claim that their work is objective.

Therefore, traditional historical practice involves encountering an oscillation between recovering an objective historical real and using the 'certainty' of this to elaborate a secure subjective identity, only to find oneself facing the impossibility of representing the real and in its dissolution finding their subjective identity destabilised.

Foucault suggests that the demand to return to the origin and be involved in the production of objective history ultimately remains located in Platonic modalities of history to which the genealogical historian has three responses: the parodic, the dissociative and the sacrificial.

The parodic takes on the possibility of the masquerade of history and pushes it to its most parodic limit. It emphasises the farcical choices made by historians as they present impossible models of what it is to be, based on the over-veneration of imaginary figures of the past. But rather than oppose this, the parodic use of history intensifies it as 'carnival', preparing for the time when one mask will slip easily into another. In this instance, genealogy becomes 'history in the form of a concerted carnival', hence the farcical, humorous and yet totally serious emergence of Zarathrustra.[16]

The systematic dissociation of identity comes into play because the identity that lies under the historiographical mask is uncertain and multiple. Genealogy seeks not to search for and stabilise that identity in unity but rather to effect its 'dissipation'.

The sacrifice of the subject of knowledge consists in that, confronted with the appearance that historical knowledge is 'neutral, devoid of passions, and committed solely to the truth', genealogy gestures towards the unrelenting pursuit of history in terms of its relation to the will to knowledge.[17] However, the will to knowledge is not directed towards producing a universal knowledge but rather 'ceaselessly multiplies the risks, creates dangers in every area; it breaks down illusory defences; it dissolves the unity of the subject; it releases those elements of itself that are devoted to its subversion and destruction'.[18]

Genealogy emphasises that what is at risk in historiographical methodologies is the unity of the subject itself, a subject that is fragile, ungrounded and liable to fragment. But two questions emerge if we are convinced by this critical account of the subject and the role of traditional historiography in providing the basis on which it can ground itself: what theory of power is implied by the will to knowledge and the ungrounded subject; and what kind of action is it that this subject can undertake?

POWER AND THE WILL TO KNOWLEDGE

Foucault's analysis of power begins with the unorthodox suggestion that there is an implicit conjunction between the will to knowledge and power, and that although knowledge and power are not the same thing, each incites the production of the other. It follows from this that, contrary to popular wisdom, knowledge is not something that pre-exists power and controls it from a value-free cultural perspective, but knowledge and power are intimately and productively related.

The suggestion that power is productive in relation to knowledge represents a different account of power to the one described in Chapter 1, where power was conceived of as something that prohibited, blocked, obstructed and so on. This 'negative' theory of power is seen by Foucault to have two major features: first, it deeply embeds power as cultural form, at best only allowing its recovery through a series of hermeneutic encounters; second, it depends upon a theory of repression derived from psychoanalysis. Foucault's point is that rather than being an essential feature of power, these and other effects of power are a consequence of it being theorised negatively.

> The fact that power is so deeply rooted and the difficulty of eluding its embrace are effects of all these connections. That is why the notion of repression which mechanisms of power are generally reduced to strikes me as very inadequate and possibly dangerous.[19]

In contrast to the negative, repressive account of power, Foucault develops his 'productive' model by examining 'sexuality' in the Victorian age, an epoch when we typically imagine maximum repression was in operation and sex could not be spoken of.[20] Foucault offers a striking alternative, suggesting that in the Victorian epoch sex was constantly spoken of.

> This is the essential thing: that Western man has been drawn for three centuries to the task of telling everything concerning his sex; that since the classical age there has been a constant optimization and an increasing valorization of the discourse on sex; and that this carefully analytical discourse was meant to yield multiple effects of displacement, intensification, reorientation, and modification of desire itself.[21]

and

> What is peculiar to modern societies, in fact, is not that they consigned sex to a shadow existence, but that they dedicated themselves to speaking of it *ad finitum*, while exploiting it as *the* secret.[22]

This insight, at once so obvious and yet so difficult to articulate, emerges as a consequence of raising three doubts about the repressive hypothesis and the operation of power:

(1) Is the theory of sexual repression an 'established historical fact'? This is a historical question.

(2) Does the operation of power in our society 'primarily belong to the category of repression'? Are negative, blocking categories such as repression and censorship the only way in which power is exercised in our society? These are historico-theoretical questions.

(3) Did the critique of repression interrupt or block a mechanism of power that had not been challenged before, 'or is it not in fact part of the same historical network as the thing it denounces (and doubtless misrepresents) by calling it "repression"'? Indeed, what evidence is there that there was 'a historical rupture between the age of repression and the critical analysis of repression?' These are historico-political questions.[23]

There are important theoretical issues here that need to be taken into account, which will allow the analysis of Foucault's productive model of power to emerge. First, methodological scepticism is used to doubt what seems most obvious and closest to hand, not because we believe that what we are is the outcome of progressive history, but in order to bracket off what we seem *to be* in the present and then to refuse to see this in terms of a positive value relation with the past.[24]

Second, in the case of the repressive theory of power, we can imagine that history shows us that in the seventeenth and eighteenth centuries sex operated in the light of day in a series of 'free' relations. Then, in the nineteenth century, sex was driven into the shadows, and repression came to the fore. Finally, fortunately at the end of the nineteenth century with the work of Freud, we came to understand ourselves as the subjects of this repression, which allowed us the opportunity to free ourselves once again. This account also intersects with another important story in the history of the West, that the emergence of repression coincided with the establishing of capitalism.

Third, Foucault suggests that we strategically ignore this happy progressive history of power, repression and freedom, suspend our belief in its veracity and instead ask: what other explanations are possible for the way that power operates on us today, and what effects might this have on how we are able to elaborate ourselves in the present? This takes us back to a historical question, a historico-theoretical question and a historico-political question. Is the repressive hypothesis historically verifiable? Is power used repressively in our society today? Have we today effected a break or rupture with the repressive operation of power? This does not simply involve replacing one fixed explanation with another but requires that one ask: what is the effect of taking another approach? With these three methodological strategies in place, it is then possible to reconsider the operation of power in our society according to a non-repressive model.

Perhaps we should begin with the obvious question: what is power? First, according to Foucault, 'power is not a thing, an institution, an aptitude or an object. Power describes relations of force, and as such it is a nominal concept: 'One needs to be nominalistic, no doubt: power is not an institution, and not a structure; neither is it a certain strength we are endowed with; it is the name that one attributes to a complex strategical situation in a particular society'.[25] Power, then, is a term used by Foucault to describe a series of strategic relations and has the following features:

1. power is coextensive with the social body;
2. relations of power are interwoven with other kinds of relations: production, kinship, family, sexuality;
3. power does not take the sole form of prohibition and punishment but is multiple in form;
4. interconnections of power delineate general conditions of domination organised in a more or less coherent and unitary strategy;
5. power relations serve because they are capable of being utilised in a wide range of strategies;
6. there are no relations of power without possible resistances.[26]

Power is everywhere, not because it is all-embracing but because it comes from everywhere.[27] In the light of this, Foucault suggests that any attempt to isolate power from knowledge is likely to lead to an inadequate analysis of its operation. A more effective examination might look at what power produces, by analysing specific relations between power and knowledge. Power produces both objects of knowledge and the subject to which a particular knowledge/object relates. Therefore it is the exercise of power that brings about the emergence of objects of knowledge, bodies of transformation and the possible subjects that constitute themselves around them. This has a major theoretico-political consequence, insofar as it challenges the foundational belief of humanism that the subject contemplates the truth from a politically neutral zone outside power.

> Knowledge and power are integrated with one another, and there
> is no point in dreaming of a time when knowledge will cease to
> depend on power; this is just a way of reviving humanism in a
> utopian guise. It is not possible for power to be exercised with-
> out knowledge, it is impossible for knowledge not to engender
> power.[28]

Foucault's point is that there are certain specific difficulties in
attempting to analyse power relations in terms of categories of the
subject that are assumed to exist outside power relations. Such an
approach is profoundly circular, precisely because the subject is not
'free in relation to the power system'. It is not the subject that freely
constitutes knowledge which is either 'useful or resistant to power',
but the relation power–knowledge which determines what the
possible domains of knowledge are, and how they can be engaged.

Power only exists in circulation as it produces local effects, inducing
the formation of particular knowledges that in turn constitute a range
of possible responses. Every specific individual occupies various positions in networks of power: mother, brother, father, sister, lover,
friend, teacher, employee, student, employer and so on, and so stands
in multiple positions in the power/knowledge grid. Power cannot
therefore be a permanent one-way exchange, it does not flow down
uniformly from the more powerful to the less powerful – it circulates
between bodies. We are all subjects of power in the sense that we
both simultaneously exercise it even as we experience its effects, and
in so doing constitute even such fundamental relations with ourselves
as our sense of individuality. Indeed, the individual is one of the
effects of power, an articulation of power.[29]

This theory of power is difficult to come to terms with. We are
more familiar with thinking of power in terms of the juridical or
sovereign model. In this model, power is believed to be invested in
an individual or an institution from which it flows down. The most
concentrated aspect of power is thought to be at the apex of the
cultural pyramid, the least concentrated to be found in the base of
the pyramid. The political objective that emerges from this analysis
of power has the object of *taking* power by seizing State apparatuses
where power is invested, such as the army or police. In contrast to
this, following Foucault, it can be suggested that if power is not pre-
dominantly hierarchical but rather takes the form of a 'net-like' series
of relations, it then becomes clear that there is no single site of revolt,
no point of resistance more dramatic than another; indeed there is
nothing to take hold of, or to use as an instrument against another.

This account has number of consequences for both the analysis of power and the ways in which strategic interventions into its operation might be possible. From the point of view of the analytic of power, such an analysis should begin from the capillary, micro level, focusing on that which is closest to us. This allows us to see how specific mechanisms of power are invested in bodies as they are colonised, utilised, involuted, displaced, extended and so on, and how particular local mechanisms of power congeal into forms of 'global domination'. This is what Foucault refers to as 'an *ascending* analysis of power'.[30] The focus of the analysis is, initially at least, not the legal system or State apparatuses but specific forms of subjection and domination. This is precisely the kind of analysis that Foucault undertakes in *Discipline and Punish*.[31]

It is in this sense that the analysis of power reveals that what is at issue is less an analytic of justice and freedom, but rather an analysis of the tactics and strategies by which power is circulated, how the body is penetrated, and how subjects represent themselves as a consequence of power relations. If it is the case that today power invests the body with a sexuality, an effect of this is that the body takes itself as a sexualised body-object, where we simultaneously find the truth of ourselves, while losing ourselves. This is not the subject simply projecting a representation of themself, but rather a process where the sexual subject is the object of interrelations of power that inscribe themselves on the body and induce subjects to recognise themselves in certain ways.

> What I want to show is how power relations can materially penetrate the body in depth, without depending even on the emendation of the subject's own representations. If power takes hold on the body, this isn't through its having first to be interiorised in people's consciousness. There is a network or circuit of bio-power, or somato-power, which acts as the formative matrix of sexuality itself as the historical and cultural phenomenon within which we seem at once to recognise and lose ourselves.[32]

There are two major effects of power: first that power draws out and induces the conditions under which it increasingly comes into play, and second the increasingly dense relation between power and the production of truth.

An example of the globalising, totalising, increasingly intensive effect of power is offered by Foucault in *The History of Sexuality, Volume 1: An Introduction* and concerns the sexualising of children in the nineteenth century. He suggests that as a result of the interaction of different theoretical perspectives in the nineteenth century, children were fabricated as sexual beings. As a result of this they were 'sexualised', and then, because they were considered to be endowed with a sexuality, they had to be watched over. This led to a situation where there was a pleasure to be found for the adults involved in watching over these sexualised child bodies, while at the same moment there was pleasure for the child in overcoming what was prohibited.

> Power operated as a mechanism of attraction; it drew out those peculiarities over which it kept watch. Pleasure spread to the power that harried it; power anchored the pleasure it uncovered . . . The pleasure that comes of exercising a power that questions, monitors, watches, spies, searches out, palpates, brings to light; and on the other hand, the pleasure that kindles at having to evade this power, flee from it, fool it, or travesty it. The power that lets itself be invaded by the pleasure it is pursuing; and opposite it, power asserting itself in the pleasure of showing off, scandalizing, or resisting . . . These attractions, these evasions, these circular incitements have traced around bodies and sexes, not boundaries not to be crossed, but *perpetual spirals of power and pleasure*.[33]

Just as power is a nominal concept in the work of Foucault, so is 'truth'. It is not that 'truth' does not exist, or indeed operate in the world, but rather that 'truth' is thought of as not being in a uniform or identical relation with the *real* of the world. Truth is 'of this world' – it is produced by forms of multiple restraint within the general politics of truth and is an effect of power relations and the way in which the politics of truth is constructed in any particular form of social organisation.

> Each society has its régime of truth, its 'general politics' of truth: that is, the types of discourse which it accepts and makes function as true; the mechanisms and instances which enable one to distinguish true and false statements, the means by which each is sanctioned; the techniques and procedures accorded value in the acquisition of truth; the status of those who are charged with saying what counts as true.[34]

Foucault's analysis of truth is therefore not one which attempts to reconcile truth with what it does not yet know, but rather is one that attempts to come to understand how it is that a particular 'truthful' discourse has come to take shape and have such a hold over us. His project is to write the history of the relation between thought and truth in terms of what may be described as a political economy of truth.[35]

There are five aspects of this that might be considered, that it is (1) centred on scientific discourse and the institutions which produce it; (2) subject to constant economic and political incitement; (3) the object of diffusion and consumption; (4) produced under the control of a few political apparatuses – university, army, writing, media; (5) the issue of a whole political debate and social confrontation (ideological struggles).[36]

In our epoch, science as a discursive formation plays an over-determining and grounding role in what we recognise as 'true' and at the same time disqualifies other knowledges from participating in the regime of scientificity. Those knowledges that *seek* to take on the mantle of 'science', such as psychiatry, psychology, psychoanalysis, ethnology and formalism, are precisely those where this process is most obvious. While these pseudo-sciences exist in a space half in the light of day, sometimes science, sometimes not having been quite accepted as science there are also other forms of knowledge that are 'subjugated' and which with effort and analysis can be rediscovered and brought back from the margins of knowledge. This returns us to the genealogical method which aims to rediscover these 'subjugated' knowledges so that they can be used tactically in the present.[37]

Struggles, tactics, strategies, dominations, subjugations. The analysis of power undertakes its analysis in the language of warfare. It is uncertain, never sure of its direction or possible outcomes, and is a form of analysis in which the analyst is already trapped in power relations. As a consequence of this, the 'analysing' intellectual cannot claim to be speaking from a position of being outside power. The very possibility of being an intellectual, a revolutionary or a radical is already a consequence of power relations, and all the intellectual can do is focus on the possibility of transforming their own thought and perhaps the thought of others.

> To be both an academic and an intellectual is to attempt to bring into play a kind of knowledge and analysis which is taught and accepted in the university, in such a way as to modify not only the thought of others but also one's own. This work of modifying one's own thought and that of others seems to me the raison d'être of intellectuals.[38]

The very mobility of power relations opens up the possibility of changes to specific formations. It is not therefore a question of being 'trapped and condemned' by power, but rather one of incorporating an awareness that an alteration of circumstances is always possible – although outcomes can be difficult to predict precisely – while at the same time acknowledging that there is no 'final' solution only continuing struggles.[39] In this context, the role of the intellectual is

> to reinterrogate the obvious and the assumed, to unsettle habits, ways of thinking and doing, to dissipate accepted familiarities, to re-evaluate rules and institutions and, on the basis of this re-problematisation (in which he exercises his specific function as an intellectual), to participate in the formation of a political will (in which he has his role to play as a citizen).[40]

So theories of possible action can only be presented as tools or instruments, in the context that a particular tool may only be applicable to a specific situation and to no other.[41] The role of the intellectual becomes more provisional, more tentative than we usually conceive it to be. The Foucauldian intellectual resists making definitive long-term pronouncements and refuses to speak for others, but tries to create openings whereby different groups may be able to pursue their own tactics and strategies.

> The intellectual no longer has to play the role of an advisor. The project, tactics and goals to be adopted are a matter for those who do the fighting. What the intellectual can do is to provide instruments of analysis, and at present this is the historian's essential role. What's effectively needed is a ramified, penetrative perception of the present, one that makes it possible to locate lines of weakness, strong points, positions where the instances of power have secured and implanted themselves by a system of organisation dating back over 150 years. In other words, a topological and geological survey of the battlefield – that is the intellectual's role. But as for saying, 'Here is what you must do!', certainly not.[42]

This expressly does not mean that there is nothing to be done, but rather recognises how one is also implicated in the operation of power:

> And if I don't ever say what must be done, it isn't because I believe that there's nothing to be done; on the contrary, it is

because I think that there are a thousand things to do, to invent, to forge, on the part of those who, recognizing the relations of power in which they're implicated, have decided to resist or escape them. From this point of view all of my investigations rest on a postulate of absolute optimism. I do not conduct my analyses in order to say: this is how things are, look how trapped you are. I say certain things only to the extent to which I see them as capable of permitting the transformation of reality.[43]

No matter how much one brings a harsh and critical fragmentary tone to an analysis of the present, the danger of being recaptured and recuperated is always close at hand. This is not the end of the genealogical approach but is the very condition of existence, because every recuperation opens up other analyses, rethinkings and strategies:

And, after all, is it not perhaps the case that these fragments of genealogies are no sooner brought to light, that the particular elements of the knowledge that one seeks to disinter are no sooner accredited and put into circulation, than they run the risk of re-codification, re-colonisation? In fact, those unitary discourses, which first disqualified and then ignored them when they made their appearance, are, it seems, quite ready now to annex them, to take them back within the fold of their own discourse and to invest them with everything this implies in terms of their effects of knowledge and power. And if we want to protect these only lately liberated fragments are we not in danger of ourselves constructing, with our own hands, that unitary discourse to which we are invited, perhaps to lure us into a trap, by those who say to us: 'All this is fine, but where are you heading? What kind of unity are you after?' The temptation, up to a certain point, is to reply: 'Well, we just go on, in a cumulative fashion; after all, the moment at which we risk colonisation has not yet arrived'. One could even attempt to throw out the challenge: 'Just try to colonize us then!' . . .[44]

This attitude involves rethinking the political. Everything is political, not because we can take charge of the political and direct everything towards an outcome which we choose, or because we must always take personal responsibility for what occurs in the world, but because the political field is an effect of interacting forces, of the interplay of power, and because relations of force are immanent in the political field.[45]

But it would seem that a number of difficulties emerge if the genealogical method is adopted, in conjunction with the account of power, truth and strategy that has just been outlined.

(1) If, rather than employing our efforts toward centring and sta-bilising the subject, we embrace the fragmentary, decentred model, then how can we project intentional actions? How will it be possible to bring about directed and progressive change in society? If truth is the effect of power/knowledge, then how can we determine between good and bad forms of knowledge? (2) If there is no position outside power, how is it possible for objective, ethical decisions to be made? (3) If the general characteristics of power are domination and sub-jection, then how can this be distinguished from the more particular experience of violence?

THE STABILISED SUBJECT

We would surely all acknowledge that at the very least a certain subjective 'stability' is necessary in order to be open to the life of the world. Yet it is also clear that this 'stability' can indeed under certain conditions become pathological, as in forms of psychosis. In expecting a definitive response to the question of the benefit or otherwise of the centred, stable subject, one is misrecognising the level at which the problem has its relevance. In terms of 'ordinary' life, it is important to be neither too decentred nor too centred, which is to suggest that in our everyday lives we live in something of an oscillating relation between centring and decentring, stability and instability, coherence and incoherence.

There are as many dangers in too much of one, as there are in not enough of the other. However, at the more general level of collective cultural practice, the issues are somewhat different. The more abstract, objective and reified the discourse is, the more difficult it is for each of us to encounter it in a critical way. In this context, the discourse of unity, of the one, of the True, of stable identity appears to be difficult to resist. This is precisely why the point of the encounter needs to be shifted from 'is this true and what does it mean?' to 'what are its effects?' As we are increasingly confronted by specialised bodies of knowledge about ourselves, we may never be able to glean enough technical information to involve ourselves intelligently in any debate at the point of its emergence. We can nevertheless always raise questions about the effect of a particular discourse on our experience of ourselves: we can reframe this strategic engagement within *the politics of discourse* where knowledge does not have to be evaluated in terms of true or false or right or wrong but rather in terms of its effects.[46]

In addition, we can make a more general claim about the discourse of unity, of the one, of the True, of stable identity and how it assumes a certain model of how it is to be, which appeals to a pre-existing abstract identity outside of ourselves. This is a model that values certainty and clarity, and is dependent upon assuming the existence of an intentional stable identity. The conjunction of this with a popular appreciation of a certain kind of realist science gives this model the status of an objective 'inevitability' which then becomes a normative measure, universalised and relocated to a de-historicised zone. However, if we abandon this, at least in terms of the epistemology that underpins it, must we also abandon the possibility of progress, of moving inexorably to the moment of 'Truth and slowly improving things along the way?

Once again, it is not a question of suggesting that progress does not take place. If we imagine the unexpected arrival of the microscope, we might believe that (1) it enabled humanity to progress to a potential that was always waiting to arrive and we are 'better' for its arrival, and (2) it brought about alternative possibilities of how we might relate to ourselves. The first possibility is framed around the question of progress, the second in terms of differences. The problem is not one of acknowledging that material conditions change or that alternative possibilities are opened up; the problem is that in concentrating an analysis on progress, a particular notion of value and a certain kind of subjective continuity is assumed. In assuming 'progress' as a primary category of explanation, we cannot raise the question 'what happens?' so effectively, finding ourselves locked into debates about whether it was for the better or for the worse.

> And I don't say that humanity doesn't progress. I say that it is a bad method to pose the problem as: 'How is it that we have progressed?' The problem is: how do things happen? And what happens now is not necessarily better or more advanced, or better understood, than what happened in the past.[47]

One can never be sure that alternative conditions or explanations are better or worse than previously. One can only be sure that 'something' is happening, and what is happening can always be analysed in terms of its effects.

POWER AND ETHICS

If power is a term that describes a series of relations which are shot through the social and cultural fabric as Foucault suggests, it is clear that there can be no place *outside* it from which one could establish an objective ethical standpoint. It can be argued that a consequence of this is that Foucauldian power is all-embracing, and the uncovering of objective ethics impossible, which leaves us in a situation where we are doomed to exist in a pessimistic world overdetermined by power, domination and subjection.

However, this argument refers back to a desire for explanations to be seamless, continuous and to operate at one level and only in one direction. The effect of my description of Foucault's presentation of power is precisely to substantiate the claim that the operation of power is not seamless. It is always liable to fragment, to reverse itself, to encounter its own transformations and destructions. Things can always be changed, alternative options are always possible, which – far from being pessimistic – is an optimistic view. Foucault points out that it can be argued that there are two kinds of optimism available to us today. One is involved in making the suggestion that we stand at the culmination of history, and that while we still have some way to go our democratic institutions and political structures are the best that any culture has experienced. However, this can also serve to act as a form of imperialist closure because it is underpinned by the idea that essentially this Western culture is the best that there is, in spite of its obvious weaknesses. Another form of optimism can be experienced, which does not operate as a closure and which suggests that while things can be changed, these changes do not have to be part of a progressive history but can be seen as enabling alternatives without a long-term fixed aim in mind.

> There's an optimism that consists in saying that things couldn't be better. My optimism would consist rather in saying that so many things can be changed, fragile as they are, bound up more with circumstances than necessities, more arbitrary than self-evident, more a matter of complex, but temporary, historical circumstances than with inevitable anthropological constants . . . You know, to say that we are much more recent than we think isn't a way of taking the whole weight of history on our shoulders. It's rather to place at the disposal of the work that we can do on ourselves the greatest possible share of what is presented to us as inaccessible.[48]

This sense of an optimistic but uncertain relation with ourselves draws us back to the question of what kind of ethics is possible as a result of Foucault's analysis. Such an ethics would offer uncertain and provisional guidelines by which we might live that would not depend upon identifying particular values as universal or transversal. It would be an ethics not concerned with the right, the true, the universal, but with love, friendship, silence and laughter.[49] However, given that Foucault's account of power involves struggles of domination and subjection, perhaps this description of Foucauldian ethics seems strangely quaint, romantic and dangerously innocuous, and gives rise to a further series of questions.

If power always involves strategies of domination and subjection, and we are all implicated in practices of domination and subjection, then no-one can claim to occupy a 'politics-free' zone, secure in the certainty of our objective position. More than this, if we are all implicated in practices of domination and subjection, then how is it possible to distinguish between different applications of these practices? Does this not leave us unable to distinguish between the dominating practices that a parent may apply to their child, the dominating practices of the riot police against demonstrators, and the dominating practices of torture/death camps? Indeed, to what extent can we distinguish between practices of domination and subjection and an outright engagement in unmitigated violence?

POWER AND VIOLENCE

According to Foucault, even though power dominates and subjects, because it is a relation and not a substance, by definition it always leaves open opportunities for resistance. Therefore, in its operation whenever power is being exchanged, being circulated, the possibility always exists that it can be reversed, transformed and resisted.

In contrast to general strategies of domination and resistance, Foucault characterises 'violence' in a very particular and limited way.

> A relationship of violence acts upon a body or upon things; it forces, it bends, it breaks on the wheel, it destroys, or it closes the door on all possibilities. Its opposite pole can only be passivity, and if it comes up against any resistance it has no other option but to try to minimize it. On the other hand a power relationship can only be articulated on the basis of two elements which are each indispensable if it really is to be a power relationship:

that 'the other' (the one over whom power is exercised) be thoroughly recognized and maintained to the very end as a person who acts; and that, faced with a relationship of power, a whole field of responses, reactions, results, and possible inventions may open up.[50]

The contrast between power and violence is quite striking. For Foucault, power is directed towards modifying the actions or conduct of others through maintaining a certain possibility of a choice of actions in them, while violence involves a direct application of force upon the body of the other, reducing every possibility for independent action. Violence is applied directly to a body, but more than this it is applied to a body which is not recognised as being in a 'relationship' that would allow it to act autonomously.[51] There is no suggestion here that one is liable to find oneself exclusively in a situation of power or of violence but rather that they are different forms of experience for the parties involved.

> A man who is chained up and beaten is subject to force being exerted over him. Not power. But if he can be induced to speak, when his ultimate recourse could have been to hold his tongue, preferring death, then he has been caused to behave in a certain way. His freedom has been subjected to power. He has been submitted to government. If an individual can remain free, however little his freedom may be, power can subject him to government. There is no power without potential refusal or revolt.[52]

There is a certain sense in which resistance to the stratagems of power is seen by Foucault as being a productive knowledge-producing, transforming mechanism; however, for him the significant aspect of power relations is not that they are bad but that potentially they involve 'a danger'.[53] The task then becomes one of finding ways of limiting the danger, which emerges notwithstanding one's position in relation to modes of domination and subjection.[54]

Undertaking such a task might seem impossible because it appears at times as if for Foucault power relations emerge independently from social practices and therefore are not susceptible to change, transformation and modification as a result of the actions of individuals. In a sense, this is a partly correct and partly inadequate reading of Foucault's position.

> Power relations are both intentional and nonsubjective. If in fact they are intelligible, this is not because they are the effect

of another instance that 'explains' them, but rather because they are imbued, through and through, with calculation: there is no power that is exercised without a series of aims and objectives. But this does not mean that it results from the choice or decision of an individual subject; let us not look for the headquarters that presides over its rationality; neither the caste which governs, nor the groups which control the state apparatus, nor those who make the most important economic decisions direct the entire network of power that functions in our society (and make *it* function) . . .[55]

Foucault's suggestion is that there are two levels at which one conceptualises power relations: first, at the level of individual action, 'intentional and non-subjective'; second, at the level of their intelligibility which can be analysed without connecting this to the successful achieving of individual aims and stratagems. Individuals do act in intentional ways for all kinds of reasons and on the basis of a wide range of assumptions about why they are doing what they do, and what their specific aims are. What makes these acts intelligible is that they are intentionally calculated; however, these calculations cannot act either in a uniform way, or in a single direction. In what precise way power is going to modify the actions of others is never clear, precisely because of its relational structure:

the rationality of power is characterized by tactics that are often quite explicit at the restricted level where they are inscribed (the local cynicism of power), tactics which, becoming connected to one another, attracting and propagating one another, but finding their base of support and their condition elsewhere, end by forming comprehensive systems.[56]

Hence the application of power is both intentional and non-subjective:

the logic is perfectly clear, the aims decipherable, and yet it is often the case that no one is there to have invented them, and few who can be said to have formulated them: an implicit characteristic of the great anonymous, almost unspoken strategies which coordinate the loquacious tactics whose 'inventors' or decision makers are often without hypocrisy.[57]

A power relation describes a 'mode of action' where one acts on the actions or the possible actions of others. It requires that the other be recognised and sustained as a person who can act, and therefore can interrogate a 'whole field of responses'. This contrasts with the situation of 'violence' where force is applied directly to the body, against a background where the possibilities of different kinds of resistance are expressly reduced to an absolute minimum.

Insofar as power acts on the actions of the other, it incites, produces and engages the other in the possibility of both collusion and resistance. In contrast to this, violence emerges out of a desire to fix and congeal power relations, by freezing the transfer of power between bodies and then intensifying the stability of whatever 'relation' is left. Because violence attempts to force the will of the one to the will of the other who imposes the acts of violence, it is not brought into play to constitute a subject in difference, but rather because difference is already chosen to be the object of a reductive attack. A consequence of this is that violence does not have to be condemned by referring to an abstract or universal ethics of the individual (which has its own problems) but because it reduces the possibilities of the plurality of what it is to be – to be difference. The logic of violence emerges out of the disjunction between self and other which ultimately can never be the *same* except in death, because death is a site where flows of power *between* no longer operate and everything is reduced to the same irreducible death/obliteration-state.[58]

The analysis of power will therefore establish:

1. systems of differentiations;
2. the objectives pursued;
3. the means of bringing power relations into being;
4. the forms of institutionalisation;
5. the degrees of rationalisation.[59]

So if we wish to adopt the genealogical methodology and combine it with the consequences of our analysis of power, truth and strategy, then what kind of politics and what kind of analysis are we likely to be involved in? First, we will analyse that which seems closest to us, as most above reproach, that which exists at another level of analysis than those with which we are familiar. Second, we will undertake our analysis avowedly from our own perspective and avoid speaking on behalf of others who are silenced by our speech. Third, we will adopt the principles of tactics and strategy, not the pursuit of a universal 'T'ruth. Fourth, we will pursue our analysis in the knowledge that our own discourse will play its part in the constitution of the possibilities of elaborating our relation with ourselves. Fifth, we will try to undertake our analysis of power by looking at specific forms of resistance to its operation.

> Rather than analyzing power from the point of view of its inter-
> nal rationality, it consists of analyzing power relations through
> the antagonism of strategies ... And, in order to understand
> what power relations are about, perhaps we should investigate
> the forms of resistance and attempts made to dissociate these
> relations.[60]

Sixth, we should direct our attention to those struggles against forms
of domination which appear to be 'globalised'. These struggles can be
recognised because (1) they are transversal; (2) their aim is against
power effects as such; (3) they are immediate in the sense that
people criticise instances of power which are closest to them; (4)
they question the status of the individual and assert the right to be
different, attacking everything that separates the individual from
themself, and breaking their links with others; (5) they are opposed
to effects of power which are linked with knowledge, competence
and qualification; (6) these present struggles all revolve around the
question: who we are today?[61]

In sum, they are a refusal of abstractions, of economic and ideological state violence which ignore what we are, and they are also a
refusal of a scientific or administrative inquisition which determines
who one is. Examples of these transversal struggles are the struggles
of women against men, the struggles of indigenous peoples for land
rights, of homosexuals against homophobia. These are overlapping
reference points on a grid which suggest that at the present time
three basic types of struggle can be identified:

> either against forms of domination (ethnic, social, and religious);
> against forms of exploitation which separate individuals from
> what they produce; or against that which ties the individual to
> himself and submits him to others in this way (struggles against
> subjection, against forms of subjectivity and submission).[62]

These three types of struggle are all linked to the concept of the
subject as being at once both subject and subjugated, as both the
subject and object of specific forms of domination and subjection.
The purpose of analysing these struggles of resistance is to to develop
an analysis of power that allows the development of a *strategic* interaction in these struggles:

> The word *strategy* is currently employed in three ways. First, to
> designate the means employed to attain a certain end; it is a
> question of rationality functioning to arrive at an objective.

Second, to designate the manner in which a partner in a certain game acts with regard to what he thinks should be the action of the others and what he considers the others think to be his own; it is the way in which one seeks to have the advantage over others. Third, to designate the procedures used in a situation of confrontation to deprive the opponent of his means of combat and to reduce him to giving up the struggle; it is a question therefore of the means detained to obtain victory.[63]

Foucault's strategic account of power is supported by a concept of 'progressive' politics which has a number of specific features:

1. A progressive politics is one which recognises the historic conditions and the specific rules of a practice, whereas other politics recognise only ideal necessities, one-way determinations or the free play of individual initiatives.
2. A progressive politics is one which sets out to define a practice's possibilities of transformation and the play of dependencies between these transformations, whereas other politics put their faith in the uniform abstraction of change or the thaumaturgical presence of genius.
3. A progressive politics does not make 'man' or consciousness or the subject in general into the universal operator of all transformations: it defines the different levels and functions which subjects can occupy in a domain which has its own rules of formation.
4. A progressive politics does not hold that discourses are the result of mute processes or the expression of a silent consciousness; but rather that – whether as a science, literature, religious utterance or political discourse – they form a practice which is articulated upon the other practices.
5. A progressive politics does not adopt an attitude towards scientific discourse of 'perpetual demand' or of 'sovereign criticism', but seeks to understand the manner in which diverse scientific discourses, in their positivity (that is to say, as practices linked to certain conditions, obedient to certain rules, susceptible to certain transformations) are part of a system of correlations with other practices.[64]

Foucault's account of power and violence and the subsequent political analysis allow the establishment of analytic and strategic tools that demand an engagement in the political sphere.[65] More than this, his position demands that once the analysis has been commenced and the operation of power made explicit it should be resisted, and engaged with, precisely in those sites where its effects are most intensely experienced: in the body itself. This is because power is experienced in the body, and as such this experience is part of the operation of political regimes which mark, torture, train the body, 'force it to carry out tasks, to perform ceremonies, to emit signs' – and which subject the body.[66]

> This subjection is not only obtained by the instruments of violence or ideology; it can also be direct, physical, pitting force against force, bearing on material elements, and yet without involving violence; it may be calculated, organized, technically thought out; it may be subtle, make use neither of weapons nor of terror and yet remain of a physical order. That is to say, there may be a 'knowledge' of the body that is not exactly the science of its functioning, and a mastery of its forces that is more than the ability to conquer them: this knowledge and this mastery constitute what might be called the political technology of the body.[67]

As strategies of power fabricate dispositions, manoeuvres, tactics and techniques in bodies, these dispositions become the sites of perpetual struggles for particular strategies of power to be transformed, reversed and resisted. As a consequence of this, Foucault suggests that power and freedom exist in a state of mutual excitement, which supports his view that wherever there is power, resistance is always possible.

> At the very heart of the power relationship, and constantly provoking it, are the recalcitrance of the will and the intransigence of freedom. Rather than speaking of an essential freedom, it would be better to speak of an 'agonism' – of a relationship which is at the same time reciprocal incitation and struggle; less of face-to-face confrontation which paralyzes both sides than a permanent provocation.[68]

It has been argued that Foucault's account of power necessarily leads to a relativising of ethics which in turn attacks the foundations of democracy and the possibility of freedom either as an ideal or a practice. In this respect, there are a number of points to be made: first, Foucault's point is that the purpose of democracy is not to get progressively closer to an ideal universal society, but rather to ensure that people who are administered, governed and subjected have the possibility of transforming the conditions under which they must live.

> Well, the important question here, it seems to me, is not whether a culture without restraints is possible or even desirable but whether the system of constraints in which a society functions leaves individuals the liberty to transform the system. Obviously constraints of any kind are going to be intolerable to certain segments of society. The necrophiliac finds it intolerable that graves are not accessible to him. But a system of constraint becomes truly intolerable when the individuals who are affected by it don't have the means of modifying it. This can happen when such a system becomes intangible as a result of its being considered a moral or religious imperative, or a necessary consequence of medical science.[69]

and

> There is no question that a society without restrictions is inconceivable, but I can only repeat myself in saying that these restrictions have to be within the reach of those affected by them so that they at least have the possibility of altering them.[70]

This is far from being a view that allows the individual to undertake any action: it is one that insists on a certain level of agreement about what constitutes appropriate behaviour and what is to be tolerated or not tolerated. In this context, Foucault refers to being against conditions of 'non-consensuality':

> I would say, rather, that it is perhaps a critical idea to maintain at all times: to ask oneself what proportion of nonconsensuality is implied in such a power relation, and whether that degree of nonconsensuality is necessary or not, and then one may question every power relation to that extent. The farthest I would go is to say that perhaps one must not be for consensuality, but one must be against nonconsensuality.[71]

This leads Foucault to condemn acts of violence such as rape on the grounds of non-consensuality, as he makes a distinction between freedom to choose and freedom to act. The freedom to choose is for Foucault the condition of liberty and freedom, while the freedom to act upon is one that must successfully negotiate consensuality:

First, there is the question of freedom of sexual choice that must be faced. I say freedom of sexual *choice* and not freedom of sexual *acts* because there are sexual acts like rape which should not be permitted whether they are between a man and a woman or two men. I don't think we should have as our objective some sort of absolute freedom or total liberty of sexual action. However, where freedom of sexual choice is concerned one has to be absolutely intransigent. This includes the liberty of expression of that choice. By this I mean the liberty to manifest that choice or not to manifest it. Now, there has been considerable progress in this area on the level of legislation, certainly progress in the direction of tolerance, but there is still a lot of work to be done.[72]

Foucault's account of power and its consequences for the subject and ethics have been the basis of a great deal of criticism of his work. However, much of this criticism is undertaken by reducing what is a very complex position to one of epistemological and moral relativism.[73] A detailed and careful reading of his work suggests that both of these charges dramatically miss their target and are indicative of an inability to separate on the one hand epistemological relativism from nominalism, and on the other moral relativism from what for want of a better term we might refer to as materialist moralism.

For Foucault, truth, morality and ethics are of this world and are constituted by the conditions under which we live in the present, which does not suggest in any way that they do not exist, but rather that they are fabricated in us and that the manner of this fabrication is susceptible to detailed analysis.[74] In the light of this, we can view Foucault's work on power, truth and strategy as no more than a faltering step on the difficult path of such an analysis.

NOTES

1. I am indebted for the title of this chapter to an important early collection of lectures by, and essays on, Foucault: M. Morris and P. Patton (eds), *Michel Foucault: Power, Truth, Strategy* (Sydney: Feral, 1979).
2. Foucault, *Power/Knowledge*, ed. Colin Gordon (New York: Pantheon Books, 1980), 'Truth and Power', p. 114.
3. Foucault, op. cit., *Language, Counter-Memory, Practice*, 'Nietzsche, Genealogy and History', pp. 139–64.
4. For a more detailed account of this, see Chapter 1.
5. Foucault, op. cit., *Language, Counter-Memory, Practice*, 'Nietzsche, Genealogy and History', p. 145.

6. For more detail on this, see Chapter 3.
7. Foucault, op. cit., *Language, Counter-Memory, Practice*, 'Nietzsche, Genealogy and History', p. 146.
8. Ibid., p. 148.
9. Ibid., pp. 150–1.
10. Ibid., p. 151.
11. Ibid., p. 152.
12. P. Foss, and P. Taylor (eds), *Art and Text, Burnout*, 16 (1984/5), M. Foucault, 'Interview: The Regard for Truth', p. 28.
13. Foucault, op. cit., *Power/Knowledge*, 'Truth and Power', p. 117.
14. Foucault, op. cit., *Language, Counter-Memory, Practice*, 'Nietzsche, Genealogy and History', p. 153.
15. Ibid., pp. 153–4.
16. Ibid., p. 161.
17. Ibid., p. 163.
18. Ibid.
19. Foucault, op. cit., *Power/Knowledge*, 'Body/Power', p. 59.
20. Foucault, *The History of Sexuality, Volume 1: An Introduction*, trans. Robert Hurley (London: Allen Lane, 1979).
21. Ibid., p. 23.
22. Ibid., p. 35.
23. Ibid., p. 10.
24. Foucault, op. cit., *Power/Knowledge*, 'Prison Talk', p. 49.
25. Foucault, op. cit., *The History of Sexuality*, p. 93.
26. Foucault, op. cit., *Power/Knowledge*, 'Power and Strategies', p. 142.
27. Foucault, op. cit., *The History of Sexuality*, p. 93.
28. Foucault, op. cit., *Power/Knowledge*, 'Prison Talk', p. 52.
29. Ibid., *Power/Knowledge*, 'Two Lectures on Power', Lecture 2, pp. 97–8.
30. Ibid., p. 99.
31. Refer to Chapter 3.
32. Foucault, op. cit., *Power/Knowledge*, 'The History of Sexuality', p. 186.
33. Foucault, op. cit., *The History of Sexuality*, p. 45.
34. Foucault, op. cit., *Power/Knowledge*, 'Truth and Power', p. 131.
35. Foucault, *Politics Philosophy Culture Interviews and Other Writings 1977–1984*, ed. Lawrence Kritzman (New York: Routledge, 1990), 'The Concern for Truth': 'What I am trying to do is to write the history of the relations between thought and truth; the history of thought as such is thought about truth. All those who say that, for me, truth doesn't exist are being simplistic', p. 257.
36. Foucault, op. cit., *Power/Knowledge*, 'Truth and Power', pp. 131–2.
37. Ibid., 'Two Lectures on Power', Lecture 1, p. 83.
38. Foss and Taylor (eds), op. cit., *Art and Text, Burnout*, 16, Foucault, 'The Regard for Truth', p. 29.
39. Foucault, op. cit., *Power/Knowledge*, 'Power and Strategies', pp. 141–2.
40. Foss and Taylor (eds), op. cit., *Art and Text, Burnout*, 16, Foucault, 'The Regard for Truth', p. 30.
41. Foucault, op. cit., *Power/Knowledge*, 'Power and Strategies', p. 145.
42. Ibid., 'Body/Power', p. 62.
43. Foucault, *Remarks on Marx*, trans. R. James Goldstein and James Cascaito (New York: Semiotext(e), Columbia University, 1991), 'The Discourse on Power', p. 174.
44. Foucault, op. cit., *Power/Knowledge*, 'Two Lectures on Power', Lecture 1, p. 86.

45. Ibid., *The History of Sexuality*, p. 189.
46. Genetic theory and its connection with eugenics offers a useful example of this; see Chapter 1.
47. Foucault, op. cit., *Power/Knowledge*, 'Prison Talk', p. 50.
48. Foucault, op. cit., *Politics Philosophy Culture*, 'Practicing Criticism', p. 156.
49. For more on this, see Chapter 4.
50. Hubert L. Dreyfus and Paul Rabinow, *Michel Foucault: Beyond Structuralism and Hermeneutics* (Brighton: The Harvester Press, 1982), 'Afterword', by Michel Foucault, p. 220.
51. In some respects, Foucault's account of power has some similarities with Althusser's concept of ideology, traced more on the surface and without any appeal to an implied distinction between false consciousness and true consciousness. See L. Althusser, *Lenin and Other Essays* (London: New Left Books, 1977).
52. Foucault, op. cit., *Politics Philosophy Culture*, 'Politics and Reason', pp. 83–4.
53. This is a danger just as relevant for the left-wing revolutionary as for the fascist, hence Foucault's warning not to become enamoured of power.
54. Foucault, op. cit., *Politics Philosophy Culture*, 'Social Security', p. 168.
55. Foucault, op. cit., *The History of Sexuality*, pp. 94–5.
56. Ibid., p. 95.
57. Ibid.
58. For a different analysis of this, see P. Barker, *Michel Foucault: Subversions of the Subject* (Hemel Hempstead: Harvester Wheatsheaf, 1994), pp. 186–8.
59. Dreyfus and Rabinow, op. cit., Foucault, 'Afterword', p. 223.
60. Ibid., p. 211.
61. Ibid., pp. 211–12.
62. Ibid., p. 212.
63. Ibid., pp. 224–5.
64. Burchell et al., op. cit., *The Foucault Effect*, Foucault, 'The Politics of Discourse', p. 70.
65. For more on how this involves a personal ethics, see Chapter 3.
66. Foucault, *Discipline and Punish*, trans. Alan Sheridan (Harmondsworth: Penguin Books, 1979), p. 25.
67. Ibid., p. 26.
68. Dreyfus and Rabinow, op. cit., Foucault, 'Afterword', pp. 221–2.
69. Foucault, op. cit., *Politics Philosophy Culture*, 'Sexual Act, Sexual Choice: Foucault and Homosexuality', p. 294.
70. Ibid., p. 295.
71. Foucault, op. cit., *The Foucault Reader*, 'Politics and Ethics: An Interview', p. 379.
72. Foucault, op. cit., *Politics Philosophy Culture*, 'Sexual Act, Sexual Choice: Foucault and Homosexuality', p. 289.
73. For more on this, see Chapter 6.
74. For more on this, see Chapters 3 and 4.

3

TO DISCIPLINE AND SUBJECT

The opening pages of *Discipline and Punish* are among the most remarkable of any work in philosophy or the social sciences. The graphic description of the death of Damiens the regicide provides a striking and stark contrast to the presentation of the rules for the 'House of Young Prisoners in Paris'. In only a few pages, we are taken from the agonies of Damiens' living death as he is publicly quartered, to the sanitised world of a 'ruled' life, disciplined by the management of time. The juxtaposition of the public execution and a time-table, events separated by less than a century, suggest to Foucault that a profound transformation of both penal practice and its object has taken place:

> We have, then, a public execution and a time-table. They do not punish the same crimes or the same type of delinquent. But they each define a certain penal style. Less than a century separates them. It was a time when, in Europe and in the United States, the entire economy of punishment was redistributed. It was a time of great 'scandals' for traditional justice, a time of innumerable projects for reform. It saw a new theory of law and crime, a new moral or political justification of the right to punish; old laws were abolished, old customs died out. 'Modern' codes were planned or drawn up: Russia, 1769; Prussia, 1780; Pennsylvania and Tuscany, 1786; Austria, 1788; France, 1791, Year IV; 1808 and 1810. It was a new age for penal justice.[1]

From our present-day vantage point, it appears self-evident that the institution of the modern penal system was so much better, and came so much closer to the nature of our humanity, than the savage barbarity of public torture and execution. This overlaps with a more general history of the West progressively embracing 'rationality' since the Enlightenment. This is a history that is so deeply embedded in our present cultural formation that it is rarely questioned. Indeed, it could be argued that it might be dangerous to call this rational history into question for fear of destabilising the hold that progressive rationality has over us, which might open up an irrational return to those barbaric practices from which we have only recently and fortunately escaped.

But perhaps to follow this path of thought too easily already opens the way to another danger, of accepting the closure of the 'rational' and falling victim to a situation which prevents us asking questions which our epoch demands of us that we ask. Confronted with this, it might be more productive to undertake a work of critical thought that, notwithstanding its dangerous possibilities, places us at the limit of the Enlightenment.[2]

> I think that the central issue of philosophy and critical thought since the eighteenth century has always been, still is, and will, I hope, remain the question: *What* is this Reason that we use? What are its historical effects? What are its limits, and what are its dangers? How can we exist as rational beings, fortunately committed to practicing a rationality that is unfortunately crisscrossed by intrinsic dangers? One should remain as close to this question as possible, keeping in mind that it is both central and extremely difficult to resolve. In addition, if it is extremely dangerous to say that Reason is the enemy that should be eliminated, it is just as dangerous to say that any critical questioning of this rationality risks sending us into irrationality. One should not forget – and I'm not saying this in order to criticize rationality, but in order to show how ambiguous things are – it was on the basis of the flamboyant rationality of social Darwinism that racism was formulated, becoming one of the most enduring and powerful ingredients of Nazism. This was, of course, an irrationality, but an irrationality that was at the same time, after all, a certain form of rationality . . .[3]

Foucault suggests that we must not allow the blackmail of the Enlightenment to prevent us from asking questions that seem out of time, even if they call into question our fundamental relations with ourselves. This involves embracing the 'spiral' of the 'revolving door of rationality that refers us to its necessity, to its indispensability, and at the same time, to its intrinsic dangers'.[4] It is precisely this revolving door that allows methodological guidelines for analysing changes in the technology of punishment to be put forward, without being drawn into an evaluation of whether what happens now is better or worse than what happened before.[5] These guidelines are as follows:

1. Try not to concentrate on repressive effects alone but situate them as a series of positive effects by regarding punishment as a social function.[6]
2. Analyse punitive mechanisms as techniques possessing their own specificity in the more general field of other ways of exercising power and regard 'punishment as a political tactic'.[7]
3. See if there is a common matrix between the history of penal law and the history of the human sciences and whether there is a single process of 'epistemological-juridical' formation by making 'the technology of power the very principle of the penal system and of the knowledge of man'.[8]
4. Try to discover 'whether this entry of soul on to the scene of penal justice, and with it the insertion in legal practice of a whole corpus of "scientific" knowledge, is not the effect of a transformation of the way in which the body itself is invested by power relations'.[9]

These principles also involve including in the analysis the way in which we enter into fundamental relations with our bodies/ourselves.

> Thus, by an analysis of penal leniency as a technique of power, one might understand both how man, the soul, the normal or abnormal individual have come to duplicate crime as objects of penal intervention; and in what way a specific mode of subjection was able to give birth to man as an object of knowledge for a discourse with a 'scientific' status.[10]

Foucault's reference to the soul is specific and somewhat unique. For him, it is not an essential substance but is rather more like a principle of subjective mediation, that is, it is an effect of technologies of power, born out of 'methods of punishment, supervision and constraint'. It is real insofar as it is experienced in the world as the point where technologies of the self are articulated, and reintegrated in the 'reality-reference':

> On this reality-reference, various concepts have been constructed and domains of analysis carved out: psyche, subjectivity, personality, consciousness, etc.; on it have been built scientific techniques and discourses, and the moral claims of humanism.[11]

This soul which in our epoch provides the lodging for freedom and humanism is already the effect of power and subjection. A certain substantive form of existence comes into being as a consequence of practices of domination and subjection, as the point at which power is articulated, induces effects and opens up possibilities for particular forms of mastery and subjection.[12] The juridical and penal systems serve as exemplars for the possibility of transforming and subjecting bodies and constituting them as objects of different kinds of knowledges: scientific, juridical, philosophical, political and so on. Therefore, Foucault's interest in undertaking a genealogy of the technology of punishment arises out of the present conjunction between science, the legal system and penology 'from which the power to punish derives its bases, justification and rules, from which it extends its effects and by which it masks its exorbitant singularity'. This 'scientific-legal complex' emerges out of present concerns against the background of the more general question what is happening to us today.[13]

If the project at hand is an analysis of changes in the technology of punishment, and it is intended to use the genealogical method, then the task should be undertaken without appealing to progress, increasing rationalisation, approaching our true humanity and so on.[14] Rather, what must be uncovered is what separates the execution of Damiens from the rules of the houses of correction. What should be drawn out is the difference between the technology of power applied to Damiens' body and the technology of power of the prison. What should be accounted for is the globalising spread of disciplinary technology from the confines of the prison to its modern lodging, between the fibres of our bodies, whether or not we have been imprisoned.

It is against this background that Foucault undertakes his analysis of changes in the technology of punishment and its effects in terms of the difference between a form of punishment based on torture and public execution, and a form of punishment based on disciplinary subjection.

SOVEREIGN SUBJECTION

The major technique of punishment applied to the sovereign subject is torture, which leaves marks and traces on the body of the condemned, and at the same time provides a public witness to the event of having been accused of a crime, whether one is ultimately found guilty or not. It is a public spectacle insofar as it provides a public demonstration and exhibition of the event of accusation, the signs of which can be never be effaced from the body.[15] Foucault suggests that it was cruel and violent, but not savage, as it was regulated and followed well-defined practices that are not directly analogous to a contemporary association between 'unrestrained' violence and obtaining the truth.

In addition to this, juridical torture was less concerned with what motivated the crime than with what happened, and in purely pragmatic terms obtaining a confession was an economical way of establishing both the credibility of the investigation and responsibility for the crime. At the same time, insofar as it also provides the site of a struggle between torturer and tortured, it offered an opening through which the tortured subject could have the charges dropped if the torture was resisted.[16]

> The search for truth through judicial torture was certainly a way of obtaining evidence, the most serious of all – the confession of the guilty person; but it was also the battle, and this victory of one adversary over the other, that 'produced' truth according to a ritual. In torture employed to extract a confession, there was an element of the investigation; there also was an element of the duel.[17]

Foucault suggests that if the event of the display of the tortured body and its public execution is considered strategically and not simply as an index of pre-Enlightenment barbarism, a number of 'positive' functions in the culture in which it operated can be attributed to it.

(1) The public parading of the body of the guilty man heralded his condemnation: 'the condemned man published his crime and the justice that had been meted out to him by bearing them physically on his body'.[18]

(2) The public execution became the moment of the truth of the crime. When the guilty man had nothing more to lose, he was 'free' to encounter the full truth and enormity of the crime. He could make new revelations, he could protest the injustice of his sentence, he could provide moral guidance to prevent others from following his path. In this way, he entered a certain space of 'free' speech, of the famous last words.

(3) Public torture and execution reciprocally connected the event of the spectacle of death to the crime. The execution might take place near or at the site of the crime, blasphemers might have their tongues pierced. Damiens was made to hold the dagger with which he had committed the crime, 'hand and dagger being smeared with sulphur and burnt together'.[19]

(4) During public torture and execution, the juridical system found the logic of its own ritual.

> Every death agony expresses a certain truth: but when it takes place on the scaffold, it does so with more intensity, in that it is hastened by pain; with more rigour, because it occurs exactly at the juncture between the judgement of men and the judgement of God; with more ostentation, because it takes place in public.[20]

Juridical torture and public execution act directly on the body of the condemned. The condemned body is reproduced in terms of the crime by way of a series of strategies where the crime is confessed and the perpetrator of the crime bears its consequences on his body, which everyone witnesses, as it is displayed as part of the public juridical spectacle.

In addition, the public execution is also a political ritual and a manifestation of the power of the sovereign. Crime is an attack on the sovereign insofar as it represents a challenge to the ability of the sovereign to maintain the *peace*, and punishment, torture and public execution are manifestations of the power of the sovereign over life and death, as it reaches to every part of the country. It is because it is a manifestation of the power of the sovereign that the public execution had also to be part of a display of this power that was visible and rich with symbolism and ritual.

The public execution therefore involved a certain kind of performance for the people, indeed *the people* were an integral, ambiguous part of its operation. Public executions could and sometimes did end in revolt against the manifestation of sovereign power that was on display. An execution that was considered to be unjust could be prevented, or alternatively the condemned could be bullied, mocked and jeered at in the unpredictable carnivalesque atmosphere that existed at the scene of the execution.

Foucault suggests that it was in the ambiguity of the 'carnival' of the scaffold that the glimmerings of reform were first heard, insofar as the spectacle of the public execution provided a potentially dangerous zone of confrontation between the sovereign and the people. This politics of the scaffold intersected with reformers' concern about torture as a lessening of the humanity of 'man'.

> This need for punishment without torture was first formulated as a cry from the heart or from an outraged nature. In the worst of murderers, there is one thing, at least, to be respected when

one punishes: his 'humanity'... But at the time of the Enlightenment, it was not as a theme of positive knowledge that
man was opposed to the barbarity of the public executions, but
as a legal limit: the legitimate frontier of the power to punish.
Not that which must be reached in order to alter him, but that
which must be left intact in order to respect him. *Noli me
tangere*. It marks the end of the sovereign's vengeance. The 'man'
that the reformers set up against the despotism of the scaffold
has also become a 'man-measure': not of things, but of power.[21]

The principle *noli me tangere* marks a substantial and significant
transformation in what is punished and the limits of the possibility
of punishment. The elements of measure and humanity interact and
articulate one another without there being any definition of the
fundamental principle of this connection, or its precise conceptual
content.[22]

So, according to Foucault, the reform movement, then, had
complex beginnings. It emerged partly out of the fear of the unpre-
dictability of the public execution, partly in response to emerging
notions of humanity. Importantly, it addressed the inconsistencies
and unevenness of the application of punishment, to ensure that the
'economy of the power to punish' could operate everywhere 'down to
the finest grain of the social body'.[23] In this, there is something of a
transition, from the application of physical pain directly onto the
body of the individual, to an encounter with the humanity of the
individual. Pain is no longer at the heart of punishment, but is
replaced by the representation of the possibility of pain, which
suggests a fundamental shift in how punishment is applied, the object
that it is applied to and the way in which it is received. These
features are part of a matrix that constitutes the beginnings of *disciplinary subjection*.

DISCIPLINARY SUBJECTION

Foucault outlines six principles by which disciplinary subjection can
be identified:

(1) *The rule of minimum quantity* which involves linking the notion
of disadvantage to the crime to counteract its perceived benefits.

(2) *The rule of sufficient ideality* which places the idea of pain at the
heart of punishment, rather than the actual sensation of pain. This
coincides with the disappearance of public execution 'which, at the

threshold of the theory, had found no more than a lyrical expression was now offered the possibility of a rational articulation: what must be maximized is the representation of the penalty, not its corporeal reality'.[24]

(3) *The rule of lateral effects.* Punishment must have its most 'intense' effects on those who did not commit the crime: 'if one could be sure that the criminal could not repeat the crime, it would be enough to make others believe that he had been punished'.[25]

(4) *The rule of perfect certainty.* The laws that define the crime and lay down the penalties must be perfectly clear, published and generally known. They must not be customary, but legislated, and there should be no real possibility of pardon or escape. This requires that a system of general surveillance that operates in parallel to the system of justice be established, and that the legal system reveal itself and no longer be undertaken in secret. In this way, everyone becomes aware of its operation, and should be able to understand the penalty for the crime.[26]

(5) *The rule of common truth.* The verification of the crime must obey the criteria for all truth. Confession is no longer the principal objective.

> In the arguments it employs, in the proofs it provides, legal judgement must be homogeneous with judgement in general. There is, therefore, an abandonment of legal proof, a rejection of torture, the need for a complete demonstration of the truth, an effacement of all correlation between degrees of suspicion and degrees of punishment. Like a mathematical truth, the truth of the crime will be accepted only when it is completely proven.[27]

The exercise of reason displaces the old inquisitorial model, and parallels the emergence of a science based on a rational and empirical epistemology.

(6) *The rule of optimal specification.* All offences must be clearly defined, and nothing should escape classification: 'A code is therefore necessary and this code must be sufficiently precise for each type of offence to be clearly present in it. The silence of the law must not harbour the hope of impunity.'[28]

We can now start to understand something of the distance between Damiens' punishment and what was beginning to emerge, not just in terms of the technology of punishment but also importantly in the constitution of the subject that is punished. In Damiens' case, what was important was framed around the questions: what happened and who did it? While these questions do not entirely disappear, new ones emerge that 'referred to the defendant himself, to his nature, to his way of life and his attitude of mind, to his past, to the "quality" and not to the intention of his will'.[29] The emergence of these questions will later become significant in establishing criminal psychology, and the formation of a criminality that will become the object of penal intervention rather than the crime itself. As a result of this, the penal system becomes a 'factory' for producing knowledge about individuals, 'a permanent observatory' that was concerned not with the crimes committed but with the potential danger that lay hidden in every individual.[30]

> We have, then, the sovereign and his force, the social body and the administrative apparatus; mark, sign, trace; ceremony, representation, exercise; the vanquished enemy, the juridical subject in the process of requalification, the individual subjected to immediate coercion; the tortured body, the soul with its manipulated representations, the body subjected to training . . .
>
> The problem, then, is the following: how is it that, in the end, it was the third that was adopted? How did the coercive, corporal, solitary, secret model of the power to punish replace the representative, scenic, signifying, public, collective model? Why did the physical exercise of punishment (which is not torture) replace, with the prison that is its institutional support, the social play of the signs of punishment and the prolix festival that circulated them?[31]

The body becomes the object of a technology of power that, rather than limiting its potentiality through torture and death, multiplies its possibilities and potentialities.[32] This represents a substantial change in both how power is applied and what it is applied to, and is part of the construction of the productive disciplined subject.

THE DISCIPLINED SUBJECT

The historical moment of the disciplines was the moment when an art of the human body was born, which was directed not only at the growth of its skills nor at the intensification of its subjection, but at the formation of a relation that in the mechanism itself makes it more obedient as it becomes more useful, and conversely. What was then being formed was a policy of coercions that act upon the body, a calculated manipulation of its elements, its gestures, its behaviour. The human body was entering a machinery of power that explores it, breaks it down and rearranges it. A 'political anatomy', which was also a 'mechanics of power', was being born; it defined how one may have a hold over others' bodies, not only so that they may do what one wishes, but so that they may operate as one wishes, with the techniques, the speed and the efficiency that one determines. Thus discipline produces subjected and practised bodies, 'docile' bodies. Discipline increases the forces of the body (in economic terms of utility) and diminishes these same forces (in political terms of obedience). In short, it dissociates power from the body; on the one hand, it turns it into an 'aptitude', a 'capacity', which it seeks to increase; on the other hand, it reverses the course of the energy, the power that might result from it, and turns it into a relation of strict subjection. If economic exploitation separates the force and the product of labour, let us say that disciplinary coercion establishes in the body the constricting link between an increased aptitude and increased domination.[33]

Disciplinary technology and the emergence of the disciplines are coextensive. Their intersection gives rise to new knowledges of the individual and the possibility of novel ways in which this individual can experience themself, including Enlightenment humanism.[34] Whether it occurs in the school, in the prison or in the factory, the disciplinary regime separates, divides, hierarchises and examines, as it simultaneously characterises the individual and orders them within a 'multiplicity' which both individualises and homogenises at the same time.

Discipline creates bodies and an individuality that has four characteristics: 'it is cellular (by the play of spatial distribution), it is organic (by the coding of activities), it is genetic (by the accumulation of time), it is combinatory (by the composition of forces)'.[35] These characteristics correspond to four operating techniques: 'it draws up tables; it prescribes movements; it imposes exercises; lastly, in order to obtain the combination of forces, it arranges "tactics"'.[36] If this sounds so much like 'military discipline', this is because in 'military discipline' we find an exemplary operation of these tactics and strategies, which reinforce the connection between 'military discipline' and a generalised disciplining of the 'masses'.

This serves as a reminder to us that it is military discipline that ultimately is the guarantor of the 'democratic' civil peace, and is always likely to be resorted to, to control the dissident masses. In these instances, super-disciplined bodies, such as the riot police, are sent out to encounter 'apparently' undisciplined riotous bodies in order to discipline them, by adopting the 'terror' tactics of the military. Military tactics and strategies are never far from disciplined bodies.[37]

The establishing of the 'norm' is another effect of the double strategy of individualising and homogenising. The possibility of the norm already presupposes homogenising strategies, insofar as to deviate is to deviate from the homogenised. This distance of deviation is measurable, quantifiable, examinable and so on in terms of those very individualising and homogenising practices that in the first instance constituted the 'disciplined' individual.

> It is easy to understand how the power of the norm functions within a system of formal equality, since within homogeneity that is the rule, the norm introduces, as a useful imperative and as a result of measurement, all the shading of individual differences.[38]

Integral to the operation of disciplinary subjection is the monitoring, examining and fine-tuning of its effectiveness, precisely because as individual bodies are drawn out by disciplinary tactics, their force is intensified and their 'dangerous' potential is multiplied. Homogenising them against the background of the norm attempts to neutralise this danger, while at the same time it establishes a space from which any deviation from the norm can be quickly identified and corrected.

The individual becomes the object and effect of this, and the measure of the homogenised norm against which disciplinary tactics can be brought to bear. More and more information is gathered on those who appear to be outside this norm: the criminal, the mad, children, hysterical women and so on. Groups who in earlier epochs had no particular specificity are specified, monitored, and become the objects of intense disciplinary strategies which are codified by being put into discourse.

> This turning of real lives into writing is no longer a procedure of heroization; it functions as a procedure of objectification and subjection. The carefully collated life of mental patients or delinquents belongs, as did the chronicle of kings or the adventures of the great popular bandits, to a certain political function of writing; but in a quite different technique of power.[39]

The power to judge, once in the hands of a few, is increasingly dispersed throughout a range of different knowledges and expertise. Judging, watching, measuring against the norm takes place across a wide range of cultural institutions: medical, scientific, penal, pedagogical, military, educational and psychiatric. However, the individual who is judged is already the effect of disciplinary strategies, which emerge from the application of disciplinary power and subjection. This leads Foucault to suggest that the emergence of humanism and liberal individualism are not the consequence of a humanity approaching closer to the essence of what it really is, but rather are effects of a normalising, totalising form of disciplinary power and subjection.

This seems an extraordinary proposition to make. How could humanism and liberalism have emerged from something so 'grubby', so restrictive as the imposition of disciplinary strategies? How could those fundamental ways in which we construct our relation with ourselves be a consequence of something as undignified as the application of a specific disciplinary technology?

PANOPTICISM

The discussion of the Panopticon in part 3 chapter 3 of *Discipline and Punish* serves as an example of the constitutive effect of disciplinary strategies. It is both a particularly intense instance of the disciplinary regime and also a metaphor for the more diffuse operation of the disciplinary regime as a productive apparatus for Western culture in general. The Panopticon uses a technique of subjection that induces a state of permanent visibility constituted by the architecture of the 'panoptic' building. It found its most intense expression in the prison, where inmates were aware of being placed under constant surveillance through their own observation of a centrally located observation tower. Whether the observation tower was actually 'occupied' or not made no difference, it was the unverifiable probability of surveillance that induced the 'automatic' function of this kind of disciplinary power.

This type of disciplinary technology has become more widespread. The video camera, which was used initially in maximum-security prisons and other enclosed security situations, and first entered the public sphere as a mechanism for traffic control, has now become a general disciplinary technology. In the city of Brisbane in Australia, the central mall area has become a generalised panopticon due to the presence of numerous surveillance cameras. Just as in the case of Bentham's Panopticon, it does not really matter if anyone is watching the endpoint monitors or not, or even if they are turned on – or can be turned on. They still function to produce disciplinary effects on all who are aware of their presence – and the establishing of such systems always goes hand in hand with widespread announcements in the media of their impending installation. They are far from invisible, even though it would be possible to hide them: on the contrary, they must be visible in order to function 'automatically'.

> Hence the major effect of the Panopticon: to induce in the inmate a state of conscious and permanent visibility that assures the automatic functioning of power. So to arrange things that the surveillance is permanent in its effects, even if it is discontinuous in its action; that the perfection of power should tend to render its actual exercise unnecessary; that this architectural apparatus should be a machine for creating and sustaining a power relation independent of the person who exercises it; in short, that the inmates should be caught up in a power situation of which they are themselves the bearers.[40]

This involves an operation of power that is *visible* and *unverifiable*, as the Panopticon is a power machine that breaks down the 'seen/being seen dyad'. On the one hand, when someone is in place of the observer they can see all without being seen; on the other, if no-one fulfils this role, the one who would be observed constructs a relation to themself as if they were being seen. This constitutes a form of subjection that operates psychically and does not involve physical violence.

The shopping mall with its surveillance cameras may only be incidentally a place for shopping, and instead serve as a highly productive Panopticon machine. In this context, Foucault refers to two images of discipline: the discipline of the closed institution 'established on the edge of society, turned inward towards negative functions' which is termed *the discipline blockade*, and panopticism, 'a functional mechanism that must improve the exercise of power by making it lighter, more rapid, more effective, a design of subtle coercion for a society to come'.[41] It is the movement from one to the other that leads to the constitution of disciplinary society.

Discipline is a type of power which comprises different techniques, instruments, levels of application and targets. It can be used by a range of institutions – prisons, universities, schools, hospitals – and can be applied to a variety of cultural objects: parents, children, family, students, the insane, the army, patients and so on; and it is connected with and is part of other historical processes such as the economic, juridico-political and scientific.

> On the whole, therefore, one can speak of the formation of a disciplinary society in this movement that stretches from the enclosed disciplines, a sort of social 'quarantine', to an indefinitely generalizable mechanism of 'panopticism'. Not because the disciplinary modality of power has replaced all the others; but because it has infiltrated the others, sometimes undermining them, but serving as an intermediary between them, linking them together, extending them and above all making it possible to bring the effects of power to the most minute and distant elements. It ensures an infinitesimal distribution of power relations.[42]

Disciplinary power and the emergence of specific disciplines are linked as they fulfil three criteria:

> firstly, to obtain the exercise of power at the lowest possible cost (economically, by the low expenditure it involves; politically, by its discretion, its low exteriorization, its relative invisibility, the little resistance it arouses); secondly, to bring the effects of this social power to their maximum intensity and to extend them as far as possible, without either failure or interval; thirdly, to link this 'economic' growth of power with the output of the apparatuses (educational, military, industrial or medical) within which it is exercised; in short, to increase both the docility and the utility of all the elements of the system.[43]

In its operation, disciplinary power leads to the formation of bodies of knowledge about, and of, individuals which constitute the basis of relations that they have with themselves and others. But what is unique to the disciplines is that they do not impose power from outside or above but rather they operate immanently through the construction of bodies of knowledge.

The transition from the public execution of Damiens to the disciplined prisoner of our epoch not only bears witness to different juridical practices but also marks the production of different criminal bodies. In Damiens' case, his public exposure was short, sharp and torturous, but today the disciplining of the individual is indefinite. It occurs not only during the prison sentence but in different forms outside the prison once the sentence has been completed. Foucault suggests that

> The ideal point of penality today would be an indefinite discipline: an interrogation without end, an investigation that would be extended without limit to a meticulous and ever more analytical observation, a judgement that would at the same time be the constitution of a file that was never closed, the calculated leniency of a penalty that would be interlaced with the ruthless curiosity of an examination, a procedure that would be at the same time the permanent measure of a gap in relation to an inaccessible norm and the asymptotic movement that strives to meet in infinity.[44]

But perhaps we are already closer to this situation than is suggested by the conditional tense used above. How much do we protest against the increasing use of surveillance cameras in our lives? Are we not already convinced that living in a situation of generalised surveillance and discipline is in our own interests?

The conjunction of a disciplinary technology, normalising strategies and the emergence of the 'disciplines' such as a psychiatry, criminology and so on serves to draw attention to the success of the prison and modern punishment. Foucault argues that, far from it being the case that the prisons have failed, they have been dramatically successful because:

1. they are the cornerstone of the acceptance of disciplinary technologies in our epoch;
2. they produce a number of defined objects that demand the further intervention of disciplinary technologies;
3. they normalise self-subjecting bodies both inside and outside closed institutions;
4. they produce a milieu in which delinquency comes to the fore politically and economically as a more easily manageable kind of crime.

That recidivism is endemic to the prison system therefore is not a failure; on the contrary, it is the basis of the necessity for constant, continuous surveillance that is generalisable to our society at large. Recidivism fabricates the existence of a criminal psychology that must be monitored precisely because it cannot be overcome, and is the basis of the 'carceral society' which assures both the real capture of the body and its perpetual observation; it is, by its very nature, the apparatus of punishment that conforms most completely to the new economy of power and the instrument for the formation of knowledge that this very economy needs. Its panoptic functioning enables it to play this double role. By virtue of its methods of fixing, dividing, recording, it has been one of the simplest, crudest, also most concrete, but perhaps most indispensable conditions for the development of this immense activity of examination that has objectified human behaviour... I am not saying that the human sciences emerged from the prison. But, if they have been able to be formed and to produce so many profound changes in the episteme, it is because they have been conveyed by a specific and new modality of power: a certain policy of the body, a certain way of rendering the group of men docile and useful... Knowable man (soul, individuality, consciousness, conduct, whatever it is called) is the object-effect of this analytical investment, of this domination-observation.[45]

The emergence of the carceral and disciplinary technology is related closely to the process of governmentality through which the governance of the subjecting/subjected individual is established. Governmentality, being 'contact between technologies of domination of others and those of self', has three meanings:[46]

1. The ensemble formed by the institutions, procedures, analyses and reflections, the calculations and tactics that allow the exercise of this very specific albeit complex form of power, which has as its target population, as its principal form of knowledge political economy, and as its essential technical means apparatuses of security.
2. The tendency which, over a long period and throughout the West, has steadily led towards the pre-eminence over all other forms (sovereignty, discipline, etc.) of this type of power which may be termed government, resulting, on the one hand, in the formation of a whole series of specific governmental apparatuses, and, on the other, in the development of a whole complex of *savoirs*.
3. The process, or rather the result of the process, through which the state of justice of the Middle Ages, transformed into the administrative state during the fifteenth and sixteenth centuries, gradually becomes 'governmentalized'.[47]

Governmentality is an attitude that relates to the governing of oneself in order that others may be governed. It is the basis of those self-subjecting technologies through which we are policed and police others.[48] Governmentality and policing are closely interrelated, and the term 'police' is an important one for Foucault, who gives it a greater range of meanings than those usually associated with it in English.

> And, surprisingly enough, people, at least in countries like Germany and France, where for different reasons the problem of state was considered as a major issue, recognized the necessity of defining, describing, and organizing very explicitly this new technology of power, the new techniques by which the individual could be integrated into the social entity. They recognized its necessity, and they gave it a name. This name in French is *police*, and in German *Polizei*. (I think the meaning of the English word, police, is something very different.)[49]

Foucault analyses this 'policing' technology of government, which involves the way in which the State is able to integrate and govern individuals as 'significantly useful for the world', by framing his approach in relation to the three major historical forms that 'any technology is able to take in its development and its history': 'as a dream or, better, as a utopia; then as a practice or as rules for some real institutions; and then as an academic discipline'.[50] In the first instance, this meant that policing was seen to be an integral part of State administration, on a par with the legal system, the Exchequer and the army. However, the police included these other administrative systems within its practice insofar as it concerned itself with everything to do with relationships between human beings and things: property, production and exchange. In addition to this, because it is interested in individuals that are productively useful even in a utopian world, it must also consider how individuals live, and to what kinds of accidents or diseases they may be susceptible.[51] 'In a word, what the police see to is a live, active, and productive man. Turquet employs a very remarkable expression. He says, "The police's true object is man".'[52]

Foucault's suggestion is not that man is a product of policing but that once 'working, trading, living beings' become the object of police, feudal power relations (previously 'engaged' by juridical relations based on 'birth, status or personal engagement') have become transformed.

Second, in eighteenth-century France, police regulations were specified and utilised by public servants as specific administrative practices. This involved the police in every aspect of human happiness and in all relations carried on between people:

> The police deal with religion, not, of course, from the point of view of dogmatic orthodoxy but from the point of view of the moral quality of life. In seeing to health and supplies, the police deal with the preservation of life. Concerning trade, factories, workers, the poor, and public order, the police deal with the conveniences of life. In seeing to the theater, literature, and entertainment, their object is life's pleasure. In short, life is the object of the police. The indispensable, the useful, and the superfluous: Those are the three types of things that we need, or that we can use in our lives. That people survive, that people live, that people do even better than just survive or live: That is exactly what the police have to insure.[53]

Foucault argues that this administrative policing had three effects: first, to bring together the classification of needs, which was a long-standing philosophical project, with the 'technical project of determining the correlation between the utility scale for individuals and the utility scale for the state'.[54] Second, to invert the traditional relation between the happiness of the State and its people. Previously this relation was one where the happiness of the people was an effect of good government; in this new form, the happiness of the people became an essential component in the success of the State. Third, the police deal with society and people as 'social beings, individuals with all their social relations'.

Finally, Foucault illustrates how 'policing' became a discipline. In Germany, it became established in the university system under the name *Polizeiwissenschaft*. Manuals and handbooks were written to enable policing to be taught, which, within the context of the institutional teaching and learning of policing, became a policy of government that functioned not only by prohibition and interdiction, but also by engaging in a 'permanent, and a positive intervention in the behaviour of individuals'.[55] These individuals were identified as discrete only insofar as they comprised part of 'a population'.

> For von Justi, the population and environment are in a perpetual living interrelation, and the state has to manage those living interrelations between those two types of living beings. We can

say now that the true object of the police becomes at the end of the eighteenth century, the population; or, in other words, the state has essentially to take care of men as a population. It wields its power over living beings as living beings, and its politics, therefore, has to be a biopolitics. Since the population is nothing more than what the state takes care of for its own sake, of course, the state is entitled to slaughter it, if necessary. So the reverse of biopolitics is thanopolitics.[56]

On the basis of a semantic distinction made by von Justi between police (*die Polizei*) and politics (*die Politik*), Foucault argues that we find the enduring problem of liberalism, a problem which is precisely the major focus of Foucault's work. It revolves around the application (and analysis) of strategies of prohibition and the application (and analysis) of strategies of production, with Foucault observing that the tension between the two is the basis of an ongoing engagement with 'government', as it hovers between forbidding subject/objects on the one hand and constituting object/subjects on the other.

This is the point at which self folds back on self as that which is subjected in order to subject others. The normalised subject is the subject that also normalises others.[57] *Discipline and Punish* is a text that directly engages with this, as it undertakes a genealogy of technologies of punishment and the subject/objects which they produce, and in this way serves as a 'historical background to various studies of the power of normalization and the formation of knowledge in modern society'.[58] If normalisation and the formation of knowledge in modern society provide the background for many of Foucault's major studies, it is because they refer back to formations whereby police police themselves and are able to police others. This is undertaken not by producing true statements about the world but by engaging in fundamental practices which constitute the domains in which true and false are able to operate.

> To put the matter clearly: my problem is to see how men govern (themselves and others) by the production of truth (I repeat once again that by production of truth I mean not the production of true utterances, but the establishment of domains in which the practice of true and false can be made at once ordered and pertinent).[59]

The disciplined governed subject is a subject that knows, and in that knowing is initialled into fields of practice and technologies where regimes of true and false are circulated, transmitted and elaborated. These technologies of practical reason are: technologies of production, transformation and manipulation of things; technologies of sign systems, meanings, symbols, signification; technologies of power, 'which determine the conduct of individuals and submit them to certain ends or domination, and objectivising of the subject'; technologies of the self, 'which permit individuals to effect by their own means or with the help of others a certain number of operations on their own bodies and souls, thoughts, conduct, and way of being, so as to transform themselves in order to attain a certain state of happiness, purity, wisdom, perfection or immortality'.[60]

Foucault notes that for the most part he concentrated on the last two of these technologies, increasingly becoming interested in technologies of the self. This frames Foucault's work in *Discipline and Punish* and his theses on governmentality, and is much less an attempt to analyse how we have become what we are than an address to a Kantian question:

> a new pole has been constituted for the activity of philosophizing, and this pole is characterized by the question, the permanent and ever-changing question, 'What are we today?' And that is, I think, the field of the historical reflection on ourselves. Kant, Fichte, Hegel, Nietzsche, Marx, Weber, Husserl, Heidegger, the *Frankfurterschule*, have tried to answer this question. What I am trying to do, referring to this tradition, is to give very partial and provisory answers to this question through the history of thought or, more precisely, through the historical analysis of the relationship between our thought and practices in Western society.[61]

This refers back to the historical ontology of ourselves which is concerned with relations of 'control' over things, relations of action over the actions of others and relations with oneself. These correspond with three interconnected axes: axis of knowledge, axis of power and axis of ethics.

> In other terms, the historical ontology of ourselves has to answer an open series of questions; it has to make an indefinite number of inquiries which may be multiplied and specified as much as we like, but which will all address the questions systematized as follows: How are we constituted as subjects of our own knowledge? How are we constituted as subjects who exercise or

submit to power relations? How are we constituted as moral subjects of our own actions?[62]

NOTES

1. Foucault, op. cit., *Discipline and Punish*, p. 7.
2. For more on the blackmail of the Enlightenment, see the 'Introduction' to this book.
3. Foucault, op. cit., *The Foucault Reader*, 'Space, Knowledge, Power', p. 249.
4. Ibid.
5. For more on 'progress' and genealogy, see Chapter 2.
6. See Chapter 2.
7. See Chapter 2.
8. See Chapter 1.
9. Foucault, op. cit., *Discipline and Punish*, pp. 23–4.
10. Ibid., p. 24.
11. Ibid., pp. 29–30.
12. See Chapter 2.
13. Foucault, op. cit., *Discipline and Punish*. 'I would like to write the history of this prison, with all the political investments of the body that it gathers together in its closed architecture. Why? Simply because I am interested in the past? No, if one means by the writing a history of the past in terms of the present. Yes, if one means writing the history of the present', pp. 30–1.
14. For an account of the genealogical method, see Chapter 2.
15. Foucault, op. cit., *Discipline and Punish*, pp. 33–4.
16. Ibid., p. 40.
17. Ibid., p. 41.
18. Ibid., p. 43.
19. Ibid., p. 45.
20. Ibid., pp. 45–6.
21. Ibid., p. 74.
22. Ibid.
23. Ibid., p. 80.
24. Ibid., p. 95.
25. Ibid.
26. Ibid., p. 96.
27. Ibid., p. 97.
28. Ibid., p. 98.
29. Ibid., p. 99.
30. Ibid., p. 126.
31. Ibid., p. 131.
32. For an account of the positive, productive theory of power, see Chapter 2.
33. Foucault, op. cit., *Discipline and Punish*, pp. 137–8.
34. Ibid., p. 141.
35. Ibid., p. 167.
36. Ibid.
37. This relates closely to Foucault's transformation of Von Clauswitz's comment on war and politics. Foucault reverses the maxim to take the form of 'politics being war by other means'. See Foucault, op. cit., *Power/Knowledge*, 'Two Lectures', p. 90.

38. Foucault, op. cit., *Discipline and Punish*, p. 184.
39. Ibid., p. 192.
40. Ibid., p. 201.
41. Ibid., p. 209.
42. Ibid., p. 216.
43. Ibid., p. 218.
44. Ibid., p. 227.
45. Ibid., pp. 304–5.
46. Foucault, *Technologies of the Self*, ed. L. H. Martin, H. Gutman and P. H. Hutton (London: Tavistock Publications; The University of Massachusetts Press, 1988). Foucault, *Technologies of the Self*, p. 19. For more on technologies of the self, see Chapter 4.
47. Burchell et al., op. cit., *The Foucault Effect*, Foucault, 'Governmentality', pp. 102–3.
48. Foucault, op. cit., *Technologies of the Self*, 'The Political Technology of Individuals', p. 152.
49. Ibid., p. 153.
50. Ibid., p. 154.
51. Ibid., p. 155.
52. Ibid., pp. 155–6.
53. Ibid., p. 157. At this point, Foucault is 'approvingly' paraphrasing Delamare.
54. Ibid., p. 157.
55. Ibid., p. 159.
56. Ibid., p. 160.
57. For more on this, see Chapter 4.
58. Foucault, op. cit., *Discipline and Punish*, p. 308.
59. Burchell et al., op. cit., *The Foucault Effect*, Foucault, 'Questions of Method', p. 79.
60. Foucault, op. cit., *Technologies of the Self*, 'Technologies of the Self', p. 18.
61. Ibid., 'The Political Technology of Individuals', pp. 145–6.
62. Foucault, op. cit., *The Foucault Reader*, 'What is Enlightenment?', pp. 48–9. For more on the historical ontology of ourselves, see Chapter 4.

4

SUBJECTIVITIES AND SELVES

There are some extraordinary moments in an astonishing and now famous discussion between Elders, Chomsky and Foucault.[1] Most of the astonishment belongs to Elders and Chomsky while most of the laughter and long pauses emanate from Foucault. This debate with its primary focus on Chomsky and Foucault can be and has been seen as a classic confrontation between two of our epoch's most highly regarded intellectuals, each struggling to capture the minds of their age in order to lead intellectual life onwards and forwards. But this reading of the event is a particular one which is very close to Chomsky's own interpretation of theoretical and intellectual practice, and is precisely the reading that Foucault's attitude during the discussion is at pains to bring into question.

With this in mind, it is possible to consider that in this interaction between these two proper names we have an encounter between two styles of thought. On the one hand, Chomsky rigorously defends a theory of 'human nature', personal creativity and the need for a transformative intellectual politics. On the other, Foucault insists that human nature is not natural but is the effect of the production of knowledge, which is a specific historical and cultural practice.[2]

> FOUCAULT: Yes, but then isn't there a danger here? If you say that a certain human nature exists, that this human nature has not been given in actual society the rights and possibilities which allow it to realise itself . . . that's really what you have said, I believe.
>
> CHOMSKY: Yes.
>
> FOUCAULT: And if one admits that, doesn't one risk defining this human nature – which is at the same time ideal and real, and has been hidden and repressed until now – in terms borrowed from our society, from our civilisation, from our culture?[3]

Even reading the text, one can almost hear the frustration in Chomsky's voice, and feel the tension as Foucault resists the interventions of the moderator Fons Elders:

> ELDERS: When you discover a new fundamental idea, Mr Foucault, do you believe, that as far as your own personal creativity is concerned something is happening that makes you feel that you are being liberated: that something new has been developed? Perhaps afterwards you discover that it was not so new. But do you yourself believe that, within your own personality, creativity and freedom are working together or not?
>
> FOUCAULT: Oh, you know, I don't believe that the problem of personal experience is so important . . . And to that degree, when I no doubt wrongly believe that I am saying something new, I am nevertheless conscious of the fact that in my statement there are rules at work, not only linguistic rules, but also epistemological rules, and those rules characterise contemporary knowledge.[4]

And, again:

> ELDERS: But what does this theory of knowledge mean for the theme of the death of man or the end of the period of the nineteenth–twentieth centuries?
>
> FOUCAULT: But this doesn't have any relation to what we are talking about.
>
> ELDERS: I don't know, because I was trying to apply what you have said to your anthropological notion. You have already refused to speak about your own creativity and freedom, haven't you? Well, I'm wondering what are the psychological reasons for this . . .
>
> FOUCAULT [protesting]: Well, you can wonder about it, but I can't help that.
>
> ELDERS: Ah, well.
>
> FOUCAULT: I am not wondering about it.
>
> ELDERS: But what are the objective reasons, in relation to your conception of understanding, of knowledge, of science, for refusing to answer these personal questions? When there is a problem for you to answer, what are your reasons for making a problem out of a personal question?

FOUCAULT: No, I'm not making a problem out of a personal question, I make of a personal question an absence of a problem ... The idea seems simple enough. Well, four or five thousand years of medicine in the West were needed before we had the idea of looking for the cause of the malady in the lesion of a corpse. If you tried to explain this by the personality of Bichat, I believe that would be without interest. If, on the contrary, you tried to establish the place of disease and of death in society at the end of the eighteenth century, and what interest industrial society effectively had in quadrupling the entire population in order to expand and develop itself, as a result of which medical surveys of society were made, big hospitals were opened, etc.; if you tried to find out how medical knowledge became institutionalised in that period, how its relations with other kinds of knowledge were ordered, well, then you could see how the relationship between disease, the hospitalised, ill person, the corpse, and pathological anatomy were made possible. Here is, I believe, a form of analysis which I don't say is new, but which in any case has been much too neglected; and personal events have almost nothing to do with it.[5]

The reader can share a certain amazement with both Chomsky and Elders that an intellectual such as Foucault could argue against human nature, personal creativity, and even universal values such as justice. Moreover, his argument is highly politicised, suggesting that the 'ideal and real' are effects of bodies of knowledge and specific political and social practices. In this way, Foucault allows that people may conceive of themselves in terms of human nature, and act in the world as if such a thing exists, because in terms of how they operate in the world, it does exist. However, the point to be made is that this is not a natural or essential attribute of what it is to be human, but rather is an effect induced by specific forms of knowledge and particular political and social practices. This may seem to be splitting hairs just to make a political point, but there is a great deal invested both socially and politically in this distinction. If one accepts Chomsky and Elders' position that human nature exists in an essential way, it follows that we should undertake an elaboration and definition of values that accord with this nature. Once these values are known, they become universal insofar as they can then be applied to all human cultures across time, and independent of their specific cultural history.

The examples used by Chomsky and Elders – human nature, personal creativity and justice – intuitively seem to be beyond serious challenge, but from Foucault's perspective this is precisely why he considers their position a dangerous one. It is dangerous, because it de-historicises these 'attributes' of social life, and puts them in a realm outside specific cultural forms, where they cannot be effectively criticised. His concern is less that people adopt certain values, but that values are always adopted and therefore must always be able to be critically thought against. Hence his response to Chomsky in relation to one of Elders' interventions:

> CHOMSKY: My particular interest, in this connection at least, is with the intrinsic capacities of the mind; yours, as you say, is in the particular arrangement of social and economic and other conditions.

> FOUCAULT: But I don't believe that difference is connected to our characters – because at this moment it would make Mr. Elders right, and he must not be right . . . It is connected to the state of knowledge, of knowing, in which we are working. The linguistics with which you have been familiar, and which you have succeeded in transforming, excluded the importance of the creative subject, of the creative speaking subject; while the history of science such as it existed when people of my generation were starting to work, on the contrary, exalted individual creativity . . .[6]

Foucault's point is that intellectuals can only operate from within the theoretical terrain in which they are located, and address problems that emerge from within it. He considers that Chomsky's response to a 'linguistics' in which he was working was to restore the place of the creative speaking subject to a discipline that had systematically eliminated it. In contrast to this, the discipline that Foucault was working in had valorised and fetishised the role of the creative individual, so his response was to efface it.

> FOUCAULT: No, I would like to say this: in the historical studies that I have been able to make, or have tried to make, I have without any doubt given very little room to what you might call the creativity of individuals, to their capacity for creation, to their aptitude for inventing by themselves, for originating concepts, theories or scientific truths by themselves . . . And what if understanding the relation of the subject to truth were just an

effect of knowledge? What if understanding were a complex, multiple, non-individual formation, not 'subjected to the subject', which produced effects of truth? One should then put forward positively this entire dimension which the history of science has negativised; analyse the productive capacity of knowledge as a collective practice; and consequently replace individuals and their 'knowledge' in the development of a knowledge which at a given moment functions according to certain rules which one can register and describe . . .[7]

According to Foucault, disciplines create the possibility for a number of responses and negate others according to rules which 'one can register and describe'. The possibility of any particular individual statement emerges from these rules, and so the individual creative act is not that which precedes the individual statement, but rather is a consequence of transformations in which the individual has no originating role.[8] There is no value or conceptualisation that is outside this non-subjective process of knowledge production.

The significance of this becomes clearer later in the discussion when Chomsky argues that justice has a universal character precisely because it is an essential characteristic of all human beings. A consequence of this is that it ensures that intellectuals pursuing justice are undertaking a task the value of which is unchallengeable. In response to this, Foucault argues that 'justice' as a concept is already part of an existing social and political formation, and as such serves a role within that formation:

> FOUCAULT: If you like, I will be a little bit Nietzschean about this; in other words, it seems to me that the idea of justice in itself is an idea which in effect has been invented and put to work in different types of societies as an instrument of a certain political and economic power or as a weapon against that power. But it seems to me that, in any case, the notion of justice itself functions within a society of classes as a claim made by the oppressed class and as a justification for it.[9]

The suggestion is that justice, human nature and personal creativity are consequences of forms of knowledge, social formations and political practices, and, as such, are precisely that which is subject to contestation. Therefore, they cannot be used to ground political action in a value-free way, by appealing to what Foucault refers to as 'an ideal justice'. Chomsky's response is interesting:

CHOMSKY: I don't agree with that.

FOUCAULT: And in a classless society, I am not sure that we would still use this notion of justice.

CHOMSKY: Well, here I really disagree. I think there is some sort of an absolute basis – if you press me too hard I'll be in trouble, because I can't sketch it out – ultimately residing in fundamental human qualities, in terms of which a 'real' notion of justice is grounded.[10]

Chomsky goes on to conclude that without notions such as 'real justice' there is no basis for a transformative revolutionary practice:

CHOMSKY: There I think that one can and *must* give an argument; if you can't give an argument you should extract yourself from the struggle. Give an argument that the social revolution that you're trying to achieve *is* in the ends of social justice, *is* in the ends of realising fundamental human needs, not merely in the ends of putting some other group in power, because they want it.[11]

Foucault's response is a complex one: first, that the issue between them is not just that from their different theoretical interests they have different accounts of the problem of human nature; second, it is when the consequences of their accounts are drawn out in terms of the conjunction between human nature and political practice that their differences become critical:

FOUCAULT: No, but I don't want to answer in so little time. I would simply say this, that finally this problem of human nature, when put simply in theoretical terms, hasn't led to an argument between us; ultimately we understand each other very well on these theoretical problems. On the other hand, when we discussed the problem of human nature and political problems, then differences arose between us. And contrary to what you think, you can't prevent me from believing that these notions of human nature, of justice, of the realisation of the essence of human beings, are all notions and concepts which have been formed within our civilisation, within our type of knowledge and our form of philosophy, and that as a result form part of our class system; and one can't, however regrettable it may be, put forward these notions to describe or justify a fight which should – and shall in principle – overthrow the very fundaments of our society. This is an extrapolation for which I can't find the historical justification. That's the point.[12]

This theoretical exchange between Elders, Foucault and Chomsky is important because in it we find divergent views about issues of which many of us consider we have an almost intuitive appreciation: human nature, personal creativity, and universal values such as justice. It is rare to find this intuitive appreciation called into question in such a forthright and uncompromising way, which allows us to draw together an alternative account of what it is to be human.[13] This alternative account is based on the following suggestions:

1. human nature does not exist in any kind of substantive or essential way.
2. what we experience as most fundamental about ourselves is a consequence of theoretical, social and political practices.

It follows from this that:

1. there is no possibility that any particular set of values will ever be in accordance with this 'nature' and therefore one cannot make 'real' content claims about universal values or truths;
2. personal creativity is not the *primary* contributing factor in the emergence of new knowledges;
3. if one agrees with (1) and (2) above, then an implication follows that one cannot speak in the name of universals but rather can only speak from one's present position in a very uncertain and certainly non-prophetic way.

When this is combined with Foucault's comments on the soul as also not being real,[14] substantive or essential, we are left with the interesting question: what is the we that we are? or more personally, what is the I that I am?

The question of the 'I' has a long history within Western philosophy, and this is not the place either to reassess or to paraphrase that history, but it can be said that at least since the seventeenth century the question 'what is the I that I am?' has become paramount.[15] There is a range of possible responses which are somewhat unfairly presented here as extreme possibilities:

1. One might say that what we are is the embodiment of a soul, created by an all-powerful entity/entities, which would be a theological view.
2. One might say that what we are is nothing but a body that

exists in the world, that has certain natural characteristics which we are increasingly coming to understand, which would be a materialist/human-nature account.

3. One might say that we are a thinking being, a *Cogito*, which is a Cartesian view.

Then there are many combinations and variations of the above positions. However, Foucault wants to avoid all these possibilities, not allowing there to be any stable ground against which any kind of theological or natural account can be secured. This is a difficult task, because in an attempt to undertake this he is anxious not to fall into an 'extreme' sceptical position.[16] He does this by referring to one's existence in the world as a material object, which alone offers the possibility of putting into discourse knowledge about this material existence. This then is clearly not a question of the mind–body split within the tradition of Western philosophy. On the contrary, the possibility of fabricating any specific knowledge, even and especially in terms of what its subjects and objects might be, is already located within specific practices operating in the culture in which we unexpectedly find ourselves.

Foucault's point is that it is as material beings in the world that we interrogate our relation between the world and our existence in it, and this interrogation can only be undertaken from wherever we find ourself located at a specific historical and cultural juncture. The danger is that we come to believe that the knowledge that emerges from this interrogation can provide a ground, or a secure foundation, on which to make universal or True claims about this knowledge and the relation that we are able to interrogate. The use of the word dangerous in this context is important because it is not a question of things being bad but simply having 'risky' consequences and effects. This is precisely why, in his debate with Chomsky, Foucault notes that the problem is not just that as a result of their different theoretical enterprises each has a different view of the subject, but rather that once this is extrapolated into human nature and universal values it has significant consequences in terms of the political strategies which one is able to adopt. Foucault's response to Chomsky and Elders is not in terms of what human nature is or might be, but rather of how the category 'human nature' functions today in our society.[17]

However, if one does remove the possibility of a universal ground that we believe guarantees our fundamental relation with ourselves,

whether it be theological or natural, this has a number of consequences. They can be broadly grouped as follows:

1. how can the 'groundless' relation we have with ourselves be
   described?
2. what is the effect of this description?
3. what kind of theoretical work is possible?[18]

It is important to understand that for Foucault removing a universal or transversal grounding does not mean that there is no basis
on which to elaborate the relation that we have with ourselves. One
of the difficulties with the terminology of grounding is that it enters
directly into the history of philosophy, in a way that may not be
productive for our present purposes; rather, it might be more useful
to think of this issue in terms of 'coherences'. A certain sense of
coherence is necessary in order to establish any relation between
terms, and although we can argue that this coherence is temporary,
and does not have a universal character, we then find ourselves drawn
to the question: from where does it come? Following Foucault, it
can be proposed that these coherences on which relations with ourselves and others are elaborated emerge from our encounters with
the cultural milieu in which we find ourselves. They are provided by
bodies of knowledge, and the circulation of knowledges interacting
among us through a range of mechanisms. For example, in the case
of contemporary 'sexuality', Foucault suggests that the production
of knowledge about 'sexuality' in the late nineteenth and early twentieth centuries made possible certain relations with ourselves that were
not previously possible. The coherence provided by those relations
and their folding back on the production of this knowledge became
an ever-intensifying loop that all at once incites, blocks, prohibits
and so on.[19]

However, different bodies of knowledge produce different points
of coherence and the possibility of 'other' fundamental relations with
ourselves, and it is in this sense that we can refer to *technologies of the
self* – and here the plural of the technologies should be noted. This is
the context in which Foucault undertakes his work in *The Use of
Pleasure*, *The Care of the Self* and the *Technologies of the Self* seminar.
All three works analyse ways in which it is possible to understand
specific technologies of self as they may have been elaborated in
other epochs. This historical concern is however profoundly based in
the interests of our own epoch, and is not an attempt to understand
how we have progressively evolved from them, but rather to draw out

the possibility of an absolute difference between different kinds of self-elaboration.

The *Technologies of the Self* seminar draws out and analyses different possibilities of elaborating a relation with oneself, by examining a change of emphasis between 'to be concerned with oneself' and 'knowing oneself'. Foucault suggests that while both kinds of elaboration are still practised today, there has been a change of primary emphasis from the Greek interest in concern with oneself to a later primary emphasis on 'knowing oneself'.

> The precept 'to be concerned with oneself' was, for the Greeks, one of the main principles of cities, one of the main rules for social and personal conduct and for the art of life. For us now this notion is rather obscure and faded. When one is asked 'What is the most important moral principle in ancient philosophy?' the immediate answer is not 'Take care of oneself' but the Delphic principle, *gnothi sauton* ('Know Yourself').[20]

Foucault makes the point that for us today the principle of knowing yourself, which in the first instance was specific advice related to consulting the oracle, has become decontextualised and predominant at the expense of the issue of concern. He suggests that if we are to recover the emphasis of the concern of care of self we must analyse what the self is that we are to take care of, and argues that in the *Alcibades* we find two meanings for the word self: *auto* meaning 'the same', but also a notion of identity, which allows a shift in meaning from '"What is this self?" to "What is the plateau on which I shall find my identity?"'[21]

The response to this shift is to emphasise the principle of the soul as activity, in the 'care of self' and not the care of 'the soul-as-substance'. It is in this context that one undertakes divine contemplation and engages with the principle of knowing oneself.

> To take care of oneself consists of knowing oneself. Knowing oneself becomes the object of the quest of concern for self. Being occupied with oneself and political activities are linked. The dialogue ends when Alcibades knows he must take care of himself by examining his soul.[22]

The self became something to write about, and, in the context of taking care of self, writing both to oneself and to others came to be of major importance, and offered the possibility for a novel experience of oneself concerned with introspection and vigilance: 'Attention was paid to nuances of life, mood, and reading, and the experience of oneself was intensified and widened by virtue of this act of writing. A whole field of experience opened which earlier was absent.'[23] The possibility of emerging fields of experience is examined further by Foucault in his discussion of the early Christian religion. He notes that while the Christian religion is a salvation religion, one of its main techniques is the 'truth game'. This not only requires the acceptance of certain obligations, truths, dogmas and so on but also importantly involves knowing who one is: 'that is, to try to know what is happening inside him, to acknowledge faults, to recognize temptations, to locate desires . . .'.[24]

So salvation, purity of the soul and self-knowledge are intimately linked together and involve a hermeneutical discovering or disclosing of the truth about oneself. Foucault notes that there were two principal ways of achieving this: *exomologesis* and *exagoreusis*. *Exomologesis* described a state of penitence that involved a series of rules, prohibitions and regulations. It is not a 'verbal' behaviour but involves both a personal and public recognition of one's status as a penitent and involved disclosing this. 'Penitence in early Christianity is a way of life acted out at all times by accepting the obligation to disclose oneself. It must be visibly represented and accompanied by others who recognize the ritual.'[25]

It had two functions: to rub out the sin and restore purity; and to show a sinner as he is. It is in the rubbing-out of the sin that the sinner is shown as they really are, that is, they reveal themself. According to Foucault, the paradoxical relation between rubbing out and revealing alluded to three other explanatory models: the medical model, the tribunal model of judgement and the model of death, torture and martyrdom.[26] The martyr facing death is the model for the penitent who breaks with and refuses the past in the act of penitence:

> Penitence of sin doesn't have as its target the establishing of an identity but serves instead to mark the refusal of the self, the breaking away from self: *Ego non sum, ego*. This formula is at the heart of *publicatio sui*. It represents a break with one's past identity. These ostentatious gestures have the function of showing the truth of the state of being of the sinner. Self-revelation is at the same time self-destruction.[27]

Exagoreusis involves a self-examination of present thoughts to 'see the relation between act and thought, truth and reality', and to see if there is anything going on there that would divert one's attention away from God. This examination of the hidden in thoughts demands deciphering and begins a hermeneutics of self that always looks for something hidden in ourselves that forms the basis of our self-illusion, or self-delusion. Precisely because this involves the element of illusion or delusion, we face the difficulty of discriminating the quality of these thoughts which can be resolved only by verbalising them to our master, to whom we relate in terms of total obedience.

The master who has greater expertise is in a position to evaluate not only the thoughts but also the smallest movement of consciousness. The practice is a verbalising one, insofar as it is verbal in its object but also turns back onto its subject to constitute a verbalised subject. So, in these two styles of thought, *exomologesis* and *exagoreusis*, we have two different kinds of practice: first the ritual, symbolic, written and personal; and second, the verbal, involving a relation to a master with a greater knowledge than one's own. Both involve a certain kind of self-renunciation, but each is quite different in structure:

> In *exomologeusis* [sic], the sinner had to 'kill' himself through ascetic macerations. Whether through martyrdom or through obedience to a master, disclosure of self is the renunciation of one's own self. In *exagoreusis*, on the other hand, you show that, in permanently verbalising your thoughts and permanently obeying the master, you are renouncing your will and yourself.[28]

Foucault's point is that it is the second practice of verbalising oneself that became incorporated into the human sciences not in order to renounce the self but rather in order 'to constitute, positively, a new self'. It is the elaboration of oneself in relation to a series of new master/experts – psychiatrists, psychologists, psychoanalysts, social workers – that constitutes who we are today, a subject that is completely subjected not in a negative sense but in terms of a multiplicity of positivities.

It would be possible to undertake a similar close analysis of *The Use of Pleasure* and *The Care of the Self*; however, the point that Foucault is trying to make here has been elaborated already well enough in the exegesis previously undertaken in this chapter. That is, by using historical sources one can construct convincing accounts of fundamentally different kinds of elaboration of ourselves. This draws out the possibility that the way that we elaborate and experience ourselves today is also a product of our historicity and of the particular historico-theoretical conditions under which we encounter ourselves and others today. This takes us back to the question raised already in this work on a number of occasions: 'What are we today?' However, Foucault's reformulation of this question already indicates a significant shift in the terrain of problem. For Foucault, what we are is not a formulation that requires an answer from within the essence of Being – whether Being is a nature, or a natural condition of what it is to be, or a fixed or permanent stucture; rather, it incorporates another important question – how are we constituted as subjects today.

The argument in this chapter has been somewhat elliptical. From Foucault's encounter with Chomsky and Elders, where he objects to notions of human nature and over-emphasising personal creativity, we have followed him through historical research used to show how an argument can be made for the possibility of a different relation with oneself that is not dependent on these categories. It is on this basis that we have seen the shift in emphasis of the question: What is the I that I am? – a typically seventeenth- and eighteenth-century question – to the question: how is the I that I experience myself as constituted or fabricated?[29] It is precisely this question that has been analysed by Foucault's work on madness, sexuality and criminals.

It does not follow from this that we can simply choose who we are in a series of self-elaborations in the face of technologies of self that determine where we must begin. This would only be a reintroduction of an artful 'Californian' aesthetics of self and become another humanist philosophy of the beautiful soul, so much despised by Nietzsche and Foucault. Indeed, Foucault has on many occasions been critical of humanism, arguing that humanism depends on the construction of a series of 'subjected sovereignties', which suggest that the more one surrenders to those in power the more one's own sovereignty is extended. Humanism for Foucault is that which in fact 'prohibits *the desire for power*'.

> FOUCAULT: The theory of the subject (in the double sense of the word) is at the heart of humanism and this is why our culture has tenaciously rejected anything that could weaken its hold upon us.[30]

While he acknowledges the dangers of failing to understand that humanism has appeared in many forms and under different guises, Foucault argues that what is consistent about its reappearances is that it serves to stand between the subject and power, and imagines a power-free zone where thought might be able to occur.[31]

It has been a tradition for humanism to assume that once someone gains power he ceases to know. Power makes men mad, and
those who govern are blind; only those who keep their distance
from power, who are in no way implicated in tyranny, shut up in
their Cartesian *poêle*, their room, their meditations, only they can
discover the truth.[32]

The humanist subject in whatever specific form it takes is always
involved in its own subjection even as it constructs knowledges about
itself. However, if the subject cannot choose itself according to the
humanist model, then what other possibilities remain in store for it?
Foucault argues for the possibility of continuous transformation in
conjunction with an ontology of ourselves. These strategies utilise the
following tactics and interrelate as intersecting spirals:

1. the principle of transformation
   a. writing – *exomologesis*
   b. desubjectification of the will to power
   c. attack on culture
   d. destruction of the subject as pseudo-sovereign by:
      i. experimenting with oneself
      ii. engaging with cultural taboos
   e. making oneself permanently capable of detaching oneself
      from oneself
   f. addressing the question: What are we today?
2. a historical ontology of ourselves
   a. the cultivation of an aesthetic (ethos) attitude
   b. undertaking genealogies of the present
   c. analysing technologies of the self
   d. analysing technologies of power and domination 'which
      determine the conduct of individuals and submit them to
      certain ends or domination, and objectivising of the subject'.[33]

TRANSFORMATION

The principle of transformation involves a number of different strategies which involve the ongoing transformation of ourselves. Primarily,
for the intellectual, transformation becomes a way of thinking oneself
differently. Within this view, the objective of writing is precisely to
transform oneself and think differently. One writes in order to change
oneself, which provides a repetition of the Greek principle of *exomologesis* in a reconstituted way. This process of transformation necessarily
involves the death of a specific relation to oneself at the moment that

a different one is elaborated. This must always involve a certain detachment from oneself in order that self-transformation is a realisable possibility. Writing serves two important functions in this context, as it requires a certain detachment and elaboration and at the same time always involves a form of self-representation which doubles back on the one who writes.[34] Foucault refers to this process of self-transformation on many occasions:

> You see, that's why I really work like a dog and I worked like a dog all my life. I am not interested in the academic status of what I am doing because my problem is my own transformation. That's the reason also why, when people say, 'Well, you thought this a few years ago and you say something else,' my answer is, [*Laughter*] 'Well, do you think I have worked like that all those years to say the same thing and not to be changed?' This transformation of one's self by one's own knowledge is, I think, something rather close to the aesthetic experience. Why should a painter work if he is not transformed by his own painting?[35]

and

> In addition, the books I write constitute an experience for me that I'd like to be as rich as possible. An experience is something you come out of changed. If I had to write a book to communicate what I have already thought, I'd never have the courage to begin it. I write precisely because I don't know yet what to think about a subject that attracts my interest. In so doing, the book transforms me, changes what I think. As a consequence, each new work profoundly changes the terms of thinking which I had reached with the previous work.[36]

Writing in this schema is not therefore a process of affirming what was already known, but rather one writes precisely to call into question not just what one knows, but how it is that one elaborates a relation to this knowing. This relation is what Foucault terms subjectivisation: 'the procedure by which one obtains the constitution of the subject, or more precisely, of a subjectivity which is of course only one of the given possibilities of organization of a self-consciousness'.[37] Writing transforms and calls into question what one is, and so opens up the possibility of what one might be in the future. This is not a transformation that makes an appeal to a set of experiences or values that exist prior to an individual encounter with them, or to an individual subject which exists prior to the cultural experiences that they encounter. There is a reciprocal two-way exchange involved in this process, an exchange which shatters any possibility of discrete sub-ject–object relations and is part of the desubjectification of the will to power which involves the reducing of the role of individual agency.[38] In part, this refers back to Foucault's statement that 'Power relations are both intentional and nonsubjective'.[39] What is implied by this is that while individuals may make decisions on the basis of pursuing particular aims and strategies, it is a mistake to assume the individual to be the principle for the application of power. But also this concept gestures towards retaining non-individual or desub-jectified categories such as class, or gender. Finally, this folds over into Foucault's references to the destruction of humanism and the pseudo-sovereign subject:

> But it can be attacked in two ways: either by a 'desubjectification' of the will to power (that is, through political struggle in the context of class warfare) or by the destruction of the subject as pseudosovereign (that is, through an attack on 'culture': the sup-pression of taboos and the limitations and divisions imposed on the sexes; the setting up of communes; the loosening of the inhi-bitions with regard to drugs; the breaking of all the prohibitions that form and guide the development of a normal individual). I am referring to all those experiences which have been rejected by our civilization or which it accepts only within literature.[40]

This is extended into a challenge to the sovereign subject as that which hopes in vain to leave traces of its passing in its discursive function, as it pretends to constitute its own set of meanings and put them into discourse. Here also lies the wish of the sovereign subject, that after its material passing traces will be left behind that will indicate its previous existence. So that when someone analyses the life/work of another, beyond the countless phrases, beyond the thousands of contradictory words, beyond the multiplicities of mean-ing, the diligent exegete and commentator retraces and reconfigures a sovereign subject, an unfolding consciousness connected to these discontinuous and fragmentary remnants, driving the hand to make these 'meaningful' marks which I have on the page before me. However, this is just a wish, a wish for there to be just that little bit more beyond those momentary presences that constitute who we are in our material existences.

This wish stands in the place of something else, the possibility of self-transformation through the elaboration of a temporary relation of coherence with those presences that constitute who we are today. This is why the possibility of self-transformation is profoundly connected with the analysis of the present as 'a historical ontology of ourselves'.

A HISTORICAL ONTOLOGY OF OURSELVES

The historical ontology of ourselves emerges from posing the related questions: 'What is happening right now, and what are we, we who are perhaps nothing more than what is happening at this moment?'[41]

This ontology is drawn out from the work of Kant, which Foucault argues had two trajectories: first, on what basis true knowledge is possible – which has become an analytics of truth – and second, the related question: 'what is the present field of possible experiences?'[42] It is from this trajectory that the ontology of ourselves emerges.

This involves two aspects: first, an attitude to the present, and second, the production of a certain kind of work. This attitude which marks our epoch of modernity involves a way of relating to reality which involves 'a way of thinking and feeling; a way, too, of acting and behaving that at one and the same time marks a relation of belonging and presents itself as a task'.[43] This attitude results in critical work directed towards understanding that we as beings are historically determined, and that our contemporary reception and repetitions of the Enlightenment draw out the conditions of possibility for what we can be today. This critical work does not focus on Enlightenment rationality but analyses 'what is not or is no longer indispensable for the constitution of ourselves as autonomous subjects'.[44]

This critique involves a permanent autonomous creation and recreation of what we are, based on a historical analysis of how we have become what we experience ourselves to be.[45] This attitude of a critical ontology of ourselves is 'not a theory, a doctrine, nor even a permanent body of knowledge that is accumulating; it has to be conceived as an attitude, an ethos, a philosophical life in which the critique of what we are is at one and the same time the historical analysis of the limits that are imposed on us and an experiment with the possibility of going beyond them'.[46] This involves a double grid that intersects at the point of theoretico/self-experimentation, that opens up the possibilities of self-transformation.

Imagine that, after many years of supporting a view of human nature, one came to the conclusion that this was no longer a defensible position. The possibilities on one's own action in a number of situations may well be dramatically changed, in such a way as to allow a range of previously inconceivable practices. These practices would then be the basis of transformation and experimentation.

> In this sense I consider myself more an experimenter than a theorist; I don't develop deductive systems to apply uniformly in different fields of research. When I write, I do it above all to change myself and not to think the same thing as before.[47]

However, there is a danger here that this process is understood as first getting the theory right and then undertaking its practice in everyday life. This would amount to a reformulation of the theory/practice split, and would draw us back to where we began this chapter, a debate about the role of personal creativity, autonomous action, freedom and so on. This is not the point being made here:

> But I think that we must reckon with several facts: there is a very tenuous 'analytic' link between a philosophical conception and the concrete political attitude of someone who is appealing to it . . . The key to the personal poetic attitude of a philosopher is not to be sought in his ideas, as if it could be deduced from them, but rather in his philosophy-as-life, in his philosophical life, his ethos.[48]

So we are returned here to the view that one's work and one's life do not exist in a dialectical relation with each other; on the contrary, one's life in all its variety is one's work, and one's work is one's life.

> Therefore, I believe that it is better to try to understand that someone who is a writer is not simply doing his work in his books, in what he publishes, but that his major work is, in the end, himself in the process of writing his books. This private life of an individual, his sexual preference, and his work are interrelated not because his work translates his sexual life, but because the work includes the whole life as well as the text. The work is more than the work: the subject who is writing is part of the work.[49]

This suggests a tentative process of experimentation and transformation against an intellectual background that stands in an interrogative relation with the present. The outcomes will be uncertain and provisional, and will in turn be subject to continuing transformations. This involves an elaboration of self where autonomous choices can be made from within the historico-theoretical juncture in which one finds oneself. This also involves the ongoing activity of questioning the present in order to free up our relation with how we can experience ourselves, in order that we may think differently, provisionally utilising different fields of experience, different points of coherence. This activity of establishing a critical relation to the present can be undertaken in part by reinterrogating the work of previous epochs, not in order to reconstruct how they experienced themselves, but rather to draw out our proximity and differences from the surviving textual remnants that will allow us to interrogate ourselves – and, on the basis of that interrogation, encounter different possibilities of what it is to be in the present.

> Trying to rethink the Greeks today does not consist of setting off Greek morality as the domain of morality par excellence which one would need for self-reflection. The point is rather to see to it that European thinking can take up Greek thinking again as an experience which took place once and with regard to which one can be completely free.[50]

To encounter Greek thought, then, is not to draw from it principles which we can use to determine today's morality. On the contrary, it is by drawing out the possibility of an absolute difference from the past that we can free up the possibility of absolute difference in our relation to ourselves in the present. It is in the constitution of this absolute difference that a realm of autonomy and freedom emerges, a realm intimately connected to the sceptical underpinning of the question: What are we today?

What we are today, are beings that have before them the possibility of constant transformation. We no longer need to define ourselves in terms of that which changes, qualified and measured against the immobility of the ideal posed by Plato, but can embrace transformation and change as a positive experience of ourselves. This involves an autonomous choice of how we should be, that is personal precisely because it is located in the materiality of our own physical existence. It is therefore not generalisable and is opposed to all universal moralities. The absolute embeddedness of how we elaborate our relation with ourselves in our own materiality draws us towards facing the void of death, acknowledging that no substantive part of us will survive the void. In the absence of life, there will be no remainder, no excess, nothing left over, neither soul, nor subject, nor *cogito*, psychology nor whatever else we might want to name those idealised, universalised grounding points of coherence that we are today. In the face of this, should we become subjected by anxiety and fear or should we embrace the positive openings which it creates for the possibility of self-transformation?

> It is understandable that some people should weep over the present void and hanker instead, in the world of ideas, after a little monarchy. But those who, for once in their lives, have found a new tone, a new way of looking, a new way of doing, those people, I believe, will never feel the need to lament that the world is error, that history is filled with people of no consequence, and that it is time for others to keep quiet so that at last the sound of their disapproval may be heard . . .[51]

This can be presented as an optimistic vision of embracing a continuous present continually being remade, ever transforming itself – a transformation that involves autonomy and freedom in respect of the limits that we encounter in our self-elaboration. It is not that one can simply be anything, but that a freedom of response is possible in any given historico-social formation. As the formation is transformed through critical historical work, so the freedom of possible responses is opened up and multiplied. A consequence of this is that we can be other than we have been, in face of an intensification of the elaboration of the work of our life as it surrounds us, laced by its temporary coherences in the face of the onrushing void of death.

> I know that knowledge can transform us, that truth is not only a way of deciphering the world (and maybe what we call truth doesn't transform anything) but that if I know the truth I will be changed. And maybe I will be saved. Or maybe I'll die but I think that is the same anyway for me. [*Laughter*][52]

NOTES

1. Fons Elders, *Reflexive Water: The Basic Concerns of Mankind* (London: Souvenir Press, 1974), 'Human Nature: Justice versus Power', pp. 135–97.
2. For the implications of this on the role of the intellectual, see Chapter 2.
3. Elders, op. cit., p. 173.
4. Ibid., pp. 153–4.
5. Ibid., p. 161.
6. Ibid., pp. 163–4.
7. Ibid., pp. 147–9.
8. For more on this, see Chapters 1 and 5.
9. Elders, op. cit., pp. 184–5.
10. Ibid., p. 184.
11. Ibid., p. 186.
12. Ibid., p. 187.
13. For the implications of this in terms of political strategy, see Chapter 2.

14. For Foucault's account of the soul, see Chapter 3.
15. In this context, the work of Descartes is generally thought to be most significant. This can be examined in one of the many editions of *The Discourse on Method*, including Descartes, *The Philosophical Works of Descartes, vols I & II*, trans. Elizabeth Haldane and G. R. T. Ross (London: Cambridge University Press, 1967).
16. For more on Foucault's nominalism, see Chapter 1.
17. Foucault, op. cit., *The Foucault Reader*, P. Rabinow, 'Introduction', p. 4.
18. See Chapter 2.
19. See Chapter 2. An example of this would be the experience of oneself as an Oedipal subject.
20. Foucault, op. cit., *Technologies of the Self*, 'Technologies of the Self', p. 19.
21. Ibid., p. 25.
22. Ibid., pp. 25–6.
23. Ibid., p. 28.
24. Ibid., p. 40.
25. Ibid., p. 42.
26. Ibid., pp. 42–3.
27. Ibid., p. 43.
28. Ibid., p. 48.
29. See Chapter 3.
30. Foucault, op. cit., *Language, Counter-Memory, Practice*, 'Revolutionary Practice Until Now', p. 222.
31. For the different form of humanism, see Foucault, op. cit., *The Foucault Reader*, 'What is Enlightenment?', p. 44.
32. Foucault, op. cit., *Power/Knowledge*, 'Prison Talk', p. 51.
33. Foucault, op. cit., *Technologies of the Self*, 'Technologies of the Self', p. 18.
34. Foucault, op. cit., *Language, Counter-Memory, Practice*, 'Preface to Transgression', p. 4.
35. Foucault, op. cit., *Politics Philosophy Culture*, 'The Minimalist Self', p. 14.
36. Foucault, op. cit., *Remarks on Marx*, 'How an Experience Book is Born', p. 27.
37. Foucault, op. cit., *Politics Philosophy Culture*, 'The Return of Morality', p. 253.
38. See Chapter 2.
39. Foucault, op. cit., *The History of Sexuality, Volume 1: An Introduction*, pp. 94–5. For more on this, see Chapter 2.
40. Foucault, op. cit., *Language, Counter-Memory, Practice*, 'Revolutionary Practice Until Now', p. 222.
41. Foucault, op. cit., *Politics Philosophy Culture*, 'Power and Sex', p. 121.
42. Ibid., 'The Art of Telling the Truth', p. 95.
43. Foucault, op. cit., *The Foucault Reader*, 'What is Enlightenment?', p. 39.
44. Ibid., p. 43.
45. See Chapter 2.
46. Foucault, op. cit., *The Foucault Reader*, 'What is Enlightenment?', p. 50.
47. Foucault, op. cit., *Remarks on Marx*, 'How an Experience Book is Born', p. 27.
48. Foucault, op. cit., *The Foucault Reader*, 'Politics and Ethics: An Interview', p. 374.
49. Foucault, op. cit., *Death and the Labyrinth*, 'Postscript: An Interview with Michel Foucault', p. 184.
50. Foucault, op. cit., *Politics Philosophy Culture*, 'The Return of Morality', p. 249.
51. Ibid., 'The Masked Philosopher', p. 330.
52. Ibid., 'The Minimalist Self', p. 14.

5

THOUGHT FROM THE OUTSIDE

In the introduction to *The Archaeology of Knowledge*, we find a comment that seems somewhat curious and rather out of place in what appears at first sight to be a rather dry, boring, methodological work: 'Do not ask me who I am and do not ask me to remain the same: leave it to our bureaucrats and our police to see that our papers are in order. At least spare us their morality when we write.'[1] Yet perhaps it is appropriate because this work serves two functions: first, to allow Foucault to attempt to distinguish his work from structuralism, and thereby resist the construction of his own identity as a 'structuralist'; second, to provide the outlines of the possibility of an analysis that is not dependent on referring back to the identity of an underlying continuous subjectivity. In this respect, *The Archaeology of Knowledge* serves as an extension to the analysis of the *Discourse on Language* and the debate with Elders and Chomsky.[2]

The issue of identity and utilising a methodology that is structural but not structuralist which frames *The Archaeology of Knowledge* was in part a response to the reception of *The Order of Things*, first published in French in 1966. This response was surprising for two reasons: first, for such a specialised book it was widely read:

> Yes, and allow me to make one remark right away: it [*The Order of Things*] is the most difficult, the most tiresome book I ever wrote, and was seriously intended to be read by about two thousand academics who happen to be interested in a number of problems concerning the history of ideas. Why did it turn out to be so successful? It's a complete mystery.[3]

Second, it was one of the works which led to Foucault being characterised as a structuralist, something to which he strongly objected, as is clear from the Introduction to the English translation of *The Order of Things*, written in 1970.

The last point is a request to the English-speaking reader. In France, certain half-witted 'commentators' persist in labelling me a 'structuralist'. I have been unable to get it into their tiny minds that I have used none of the methods, concepts, or key terms that characterise structural analysis. I should be grateful if a more serious public would free me from a connection that certainly does me honour, but that I have not deserved. There may well be certain similarities between the works of structuralists and my own work. It would hardly behove me, of all people, to claim that my discourse is independent of conditions and rules of which I am very largely unaware, and which determines other work that is being done today. But it is only too easy to avoid the trouble of analysing such work by giving it an admittedly impressive-sounding, but inaccurate label.[4]

Foucault's anger was directed towards those whose read his book through the 'structuralist' grid and failed to distinguish the difference between *structuralism* and a structural style of analysis. In hindsight, one can see how the problem that Foucault was attempting to deal with in *The Order of Things* could have led to a 'structuralist' interpretation of his work, because in it Foucault wanted to disallow the view that the individual creative subject had a continuous structure or content and was autonomous in the production of knowledge, by historicising the interaction between the production of subjects and bodies of knowledge.

It is Foucault's insistence on the historical dimension of knowledge and his refusal to appeal to any transversal, universal or continuously grounded principles (either subject or discursive) that distinguishes his project in *The Order of Things* from both classical structuralism and the conjunction of psychoanalysis and structuralism in the work of Jacques Lacan.[5] However, it is precisely this refusal that makes the project so difficult, in that if one abandons the continuity or permanence of all of the categories usually used to provide coherence to the object of analysis, from where does the fundamental stability and coherence needed to undertake analytic work appear?

One possibility would be to bracket off a chronological period, and then examine the rules that govern the emergence of particular discourses in that epoch.[6] These rules become the precondition or condition of possibility for any particular individual discourse, which then emerges as a particular *event* within the specific constellation of discourse. It is precisely the concept of the event that Foucault used to distinguish his work in *The Order of Things* from classical structuralism:

> One can agree that structuralism formed the most systematic effort to evacuate the concept of the event, not only from ethnology but from a whole series of other sciences and in the extreme case from history. In that sense, I don't see who could be more of an anti-structuralist than myself.[7]

Foucault uses the concept of the event for two purposes: first, to historicise the event by suggesting that it is a specific historical moment within a history of the interaction between subject and discourse; second, to introduce a multi-layered analysis into the methodology. While the concept of the event can be indeed seen as anti-structuralist insofar as it attacks any attempt to de-historicise the specific emergence of discourse, the use of a multi-layered analysis at first sight may seem to draw one back to classical structuralism. However, this aspect of *The Order of Things*, which no doubt contributed to it being read as a structuralist work, is dependent on a particular reading of the concept of 'level'.

The term 'level' implies a relation between things which is conventionally thought of in terms of upper and lower, of discrete entities divided by horizontal lines. But it is also possible to think of levels in terms of geological strata, not simply and cleanly bisected by horizontal lines, but curved, compressed, extended and generally fuzzy and confused. Not only this, but there does not have to be any implication that this engagement with different levels involves the hermeneutic possibility of getting closer to some enduring truth. Imagine turning the levels (or strata) on their side. In this instance, analysing the different levels would not take you closer to or further from the truth; it would just allow a particular analysis of a specifically constituted moment in time. This is the effect of Foucault's analysis in *The Order of Things*, which shows that 'truth' and 'history' are results of the interaction between subject and discourse.[8]

> Each society has its régime of truth, its 'general politics' of truth: that is, the types of discourse which it accepts and makes function as true; the mechanisms and instances which enable one to distinguish true and false statements, the means by which each is sanctioned; the techniques and procedures accorded value in the acquisition of truth; the status of those who are charged with saying what counts as true.[9]

There are two sets of relations in *The Order of Things*: those between subject and knowledge, and those that constitute the possibilities of knowledge in the epoch under analysis. Order emerges out of the analytic 'glance' which reveals the relational grid through which language, knowledge and subject encounter each other. What can be said, what is recognisable as legitimate, is already part of the condition of possibility that knowledge as a discursive formation opens up. So the subject that interacts with bodies of knowledge is already the object of the rules of formation of knowledge in any particular epoch:

> unknown to themselves, the naturalists, economists, grammarians employed the same rules to define the objects proper to their own study, to form their concepts, to build their theories. It is these rules of formation, which were never formulated in their own right, but are to be found only in widely differing theories, concepts, and objects of study, that I have tried to reveal, by isolating, at their specific locus, a level that I have called, somewhat arbitrarily perhaps, archaeological.[10]

Foucault is careful to allow other kinds of methodological approach, such as intellectual biography, the history of theories and themes and so on; rather, his point is that in themselves each of them may not provide the whole explanation. Indeed, while noting his personal rejection of the phenomenological method, he suggests the value of others using different methods, arguing that because the investigated object is complex it requires a multi-dimensional approach: 'Discourse in general, and scientific discourse in particular, is so complex a reality that we not only can, but should, approach it at different levels and with different methods'.[11]

In suggesting the benefit of an approach with different levels and methods, Foucault incorporates into his theorising a relativising of his own methodology, and a refusal to argue that there is a single structure that would overdetermine all possible meanings. When this is combined with the view that his project is fundamentally historical, insofar as its object is always the 'history' that a discipline has taken on for itself in the present, we can find a basis for rejecting any naïve claims that Foucault is a structuralist.[12]

Foucault's *archaeological* strategy isolates its object by forcing the methodological suspension of a number of familiar concepts from the history of ideas. These include: (1) tradition; (2) influence; (3) development and evolution; (4) spirit; (5) pre-given unities and links; (6) familiar divisions and groupings; (7) the *œuvre*; (8) two interlinked themes: the irruption of the real event and the already said.[13] This allows the emergence of statements as a discontinuous irruption in discourse that questions their certainty and unity:

> The frontiers of a book are never clear-cut: beyond the title, the first lines, and the last full stop, beyond its internal configuration and its autonomous form, it is caught up in a system of references to other books, other texts, other sentences: it is a node within a network. And this network of references is not the same in the case of a mathematical treatise, a textual commentary, a historical account, and an episode in a novel cycle; the unity of the book, even in the sense of a group of relations, cannot be regarded as identical in each case. The book is not simply the object that one holds in one's hands; and it cannot remain within the little parallelepiped that contains it: its unity is variable and relative. As soon as one questions that unity, it loses its self-evidence; it indicates itself, constructs itself, only on the basis of a complex field of discourse.[14]

The suspension of pre-given unities allows for the examination of the emergence of the statement from within the 'complex field of discourse'. At the point of this emergence, aspects of the non-discursive regime, such as 'institutions, political events, economic practices and processes', also come into focus.

In this way, archaeology attempts to present a description of the possibility of statements from within discourse, which is already part of all those institutions and practices that exist at any one time. It does not seek to give meaning to the statements in some ideal, idealised way, but rather sees meaning as emerging from within specific historical formations. In this sense, it is profoundly historical and will not allow the subject to be presented ahistorically as the ground on which a particular statement is possible, but historicises the subjective ground as part of its practice.

> Discourse, at least as analysed by archaeology, that is, at the level of its positivity, is not a consciousness that embodies its project in the external form of language (*langage*); it is not a language (*langue*), plus a subject to speak it. It is a practice that has its own forms of sequence and succession.[15]

According to Foucault, subjects emerge from discourse and, because they do not pre-exist it, cannot be the basis of any foundational subjective interpretation. In contrast to those practices that depend upon continuities, unities and continuous foundations, archaeology attempts 'to untie all those knots that historians have patiently tied: it increases differences, blurs the lines of communication, and tries to make it more difficult to pass from one thing to another...'.[16] The effect of archaeology is to refuse to reduce differences to continuous forms, but rather to elaborate them, analyse them and propose how they function in the production of knowledge(s), in the differentiated spaces which knowledge allows to be deployed. The possibilities for subject, statement, discourse and non-discursive practices emerge from these differentiated spaces.

> Knowledge is that of which one can speak in a discursive prac-
> tice, and which is specified by that fact: ... knowledge is also
> the space in which the subject may take up a position and speak
> of the objects with which he deals in his discourse ... knowledge
> is also the field of coordination and subordination of statements
> in which concepts appear, and are defined, applied and trans-
> formed ... There are bodies of knowledge that are independent
> of the sciences (which are neither their historical prototypes,
> nor their practical by-products), but there is no knowledge
> without a particular discursive practice; and any discursive prac-
> tice may be defined by the knowledge that it forms. Instead
> of exploring the consciousness/knowledge (*connaissance*)/science
> axis (which cannot escape subjectivity), archaeology explores
> the discursive practice/knowledge (*savoir*)/science axis. And
> whereas the history of ideas finds the point of balance of its
> analysis in the element of *connaissance* (and is thus forced,
> against its will, to encounter the transcendental interrogation),
> archaeology finds the point of balance of its analysis in *savoir* –
> that is, in a domain in which the subject is necessarily situated
> and dependent, and can never figure as titular (either as a tran-
> scendental activity, or as empirical consciousness).[17]

Foucault's archaeological analysis is an attempt to reconstruct the ordering of knowledge in any given epoch so that the understanding of the possibility for the emergence of any particular statement can be recognised. This ordering of knowledge was referred to as the epistemological field or *episteme*, and it was the use of this term *episteme* in *The Order of Things* that gave additional support to those who wanted to read Foucault as a kind of structuralist.

> what I am attempting to bring to light is the epistemological
> field, the *episteme* in which knowledge, envisaged apart from all

criteria having reference to its rational value or to its objective forms, grounds its positivity and therefore manifests a history which is not that of its growing perfection, but rather that of its conditions of possibility; in this account, what should appear are those configurations within the *space* of knowledge which have given rise to the diverse forms of empirical science. Such an enterprise is not so much a history, in the traditional meaning of that word, as an 'archaeology'.[18]

The *episteme* is that which grounds knowledge and allows certain kinds of knowledge to assume validity and acceptance within the '*space* of knowledge'. According to the Foucault of *The Order of Things*, 'In any given culture and at any given moment, there is always only one *episteme* that defines the conditions of possibility of all knowledge, whether expressed in a theory or silently invested in a practice'.[19] The suggestion that there was only one *episteme* 'at any given moment' looked very much like the space of knowledge overdetermined the possibility of any particular encounter with it, and at first glance seems similar to the classical structuralism of Lévi-Strauss in *The Raw and the Cooked*. One could examine this work of Lévi-Strauss and argue that the *episteme* under study was based on the binary opposition between raw and cooked, and that these twin terms and their interrelation provided the entire basis for decoding all meaning and all relations.

There are a number of points to be made in relation to this. First, clearly Foucault had made a substantial error in suggesting that there could be only one *episteme* covering all forms of knowledge in any given epoch. He became well aware of this error, and this led him subsequently to modify, although not entirely abandon, the concept of the *episteme*.

> In seeking in *The Order of Things* to write a history of the *episteme*, I was still caught in an impasse. What I should like to do now is to try and show that what I called an apparatus is a much more general case of the *episteme*; or rather, that the *episteme* is a specifically discursive apparatus, whereas the apparatus in its general form is both discursive and non-discursive, its elements being much more heterogeneous.[20]

> If you like, I would define the *episteme* retrospectively as the strategic apparatus which permits of separating out from among all the statements which are possible those that will be acceptable within, I won't say a scientific theory, but a field of scientificity,

and which it is possible to say are true or false. The *episteme* is
the 'apparatus' which makes possible the separation, not of the
true from the false, but of what may form what may not be
characteristic as scientific.[21]

the *episteme* is not *a sort of grand underlying theory*, it is a space
of *dispersion*, it is an open and *doubtless indefinitely describable
field of relationships* . . . *The episteme is not a general developmental
stage of reason, it is a complex relationship of successive displacements.*[22]

In this modified form, the *episteme* loses its all-embracing totalising
position and becomes a discursive apparatus among other apparatuses which allows the scientific to be distinguished from other
forms of knowledge. The position of the *episteme* in Foucault's work
is somewhat ambiguous, and insofar as the *episteme* remains a useful
methodological tool at all, it be can used to define the conditions
under which a particular discursive formation takes its specific form.

Second, even allowing for this later modification of his own
thought, in the early elaboration of the *episteme* Foucault still avoids
the transversal, universalising claims of structuralism by historicising
the emergence of the *episteme* and tying it to a particular set of
historical conditions. This allows a clear distinction to be made
between archaeology and structuralism.

Third, Foucault does not deny the role of the individual subject,
only that they do not have 'infinite' autonomy in what they are able
to say if it is to be accepted within a particular discourse (such as
scientific discourse), where the conditions of possibility of the 'what
can be said' may overwhelm them entirely, perhaps even silence
them. In this respect, it is worth drawing attention to something
often overlooked in discussions of *The Order of Things*, that is, in this
work Foucault is attempting to describe the emergence of the human
sciences from out of the general field of scientific discourse. The
subtitle to *The Order of Things* is *An Archaeology of the Human Sciences*.
The project is to analyse how it was possible that the human sciences
emerged out of the general field of science between the seventeenth
and nineteenth centuries. In spite of the fact that their object was
quite different, that is, 'man' (not the world/universe of objects), they
still managed to present and sustain themselves as empirical sciences.
It is this sense of 'man' as only a recent object of study that Foucault
used to suggest that, just as this object is only a recent invention,
when knowledge takes different forms and different objects in the
future, it may well disappear.

If those arrangements were to disappear as they appeared, if some event of which we can at the moment do no more than sense the possibility – without knowing either what its form will be or what it promises – were to cause them to crumble, as the ground of Classical thought did, at the end of the eighteenth century, then one can certainly wager that man would be erased, like a face drawn in sand at the edge of the sea.[23]

This moment of erasure does not refer to the absence of human bodies, but only to 'man' as a specific object of study constructed in the human sciences, although it does not preclude the idea that in the absence of 'man' our experience of ourselves might indeed be quite different from how we experience and elaborate ourselves today.[24] Historicising that experience is both the aim of archaeology and its effect.

The Archaeology of Knowledge presents us with an extended 'spiralling' rumination on the word 'archaeology' whose aim is 'in short, to give meaning to the word *archaeology*, which I had so far left empty'.[25] It does this by attempting to construct its own operative theoretical space by distinguishing itself from other historical practices/methodologies within the context of two contemporary attitudes to historical practice.

First, the approach that focuses on long periods and analyses themes below the surface of political events: 'the history of sea routes, the history of corn or of gold-mining, the history of drought and of irrigation, the history of crop rotation, the history of the balance achieved by the human species between hunger and abundance'.[26] This has led to a shift in the kind of methodological questions that the practice brings forth from

> The old questions of the traditional analysis. (What link should be made between disparate events? How can a causal succession be established between them? What continuity or overall significance do they possess? Is it possible to define a totality, or must one be content with reconstituting connexions?)

to

> which strata should be isolated from others? What types of series should be established? What criteria of periodization should be adopted for each of them? What system of relations (hierarchy, dominance, stratification, univocal determination, circular causality) may be established between them? What series of series may be established? And in what large-scale

chronological table may distinct series of events be determined?[27]

Second, in contrast to this, disciplines such as the history of ideas, the history of science, the history of philosophy, the history of thought, and the history of literature have turned away from the 'vast unities like "periods" or "centuries"' to the phenomenon of rupture, of discontinuity, which has led to different questions being asked:

> how is one to specify the different concepts that enable us to conceive of discontinuity (threshold, rupture, break, mutation, transformation)? By what criteria is one to isolate the unities with which one is dealing; what is *a* science? What is an *œuvre*? What is *a* theory? What is *a* concept? What is *a* text? How is one to diversify the levels at which one may place oneself, each of which possesses its own divisions and form of analysis? What is the legitimate level of formalization? What is that of interpretation? Of structural analysis? Of attributions of causality?
>
> In short, the history of thought, of knowledge, of philosophy, of literature seems to be seeking, and discovering, more and more discontinuities, whereas history itself appears to be abandoning the irruption of events in favour of stable structures.[28]

However, Foucault does not wish simply to suggest that some historical disciplines have moved from the continuous to the discontinuous and others from the discontinuous to the continuous. Rather, his point is that both approaches lead to the posing of the same problem: 'the *questioning* of the document'. Why is 'the *questioning* of the document' something to be thought of as a problem? Because, according to Foucault, the kinds of questions posed by the document to traditional historians are: what do they mean, are they truthful, are they authentic gestures towards 'the language of a voice since reduced to silence, its fragile, but possibly decipherable trace'?[29]

In contrast to this, contemporary history does not attempt to interpret the document or discover its authenticity or truthfulness but organises it, 'divides it up, distributes it, orders it, arranges it in levels, establishes series, distinguishes between what is relevant and what is not, discovers elements, defines unities, describes relations'.[30] However, what is not recognised in this process is that the document is not that which makes this kind of history possible, simply organising a pre-existing historical memory, but rather it is the operation of the methodology of history that makes possible the form of the document and the possibility of this memory.

To be brief, then, let us say that history, in its traditional form, undertook to 'memorize' the *monuments* of the past, transform them into *documents*, and lend speech to those traces which, in themselves, are often not verbal, or which say in silence something other than what they actually say; in our time, history is that which transforms *documents* into *monuments*. In that area where, in the past, history deciphered the traces left by men, it now deploys a mass of elements that have to be grouped, made relevant, placed in relation to one another to form totalities.[31]

This contemporary approach has a number of consequences: first, it is faced with the problem of discontinuity and the construction of a coherent series which has led to the emergence of long historical periods; second, whereas in traditional history the objective was to remove or eliminate discontinuities, contemporary history now embraces discontinuity which has become one of its major theoretical vehicles. Third, the possibility of a *total history* disappears, to be replaced by *general history*.

The project of total history is one that seeks to reconstitute the overall form of a civilization, the principle – material or spiritual – of a society, the significance common to all the phenomena of a period, the law that accounts for their cohesion – what is called metaphorically the 'face' of a period.[32]

In contrast to this, for *general history*,

The problem that now presents itself – and which defines the task of general history – is to determine what form of relation may be legitimately described between these different series; what vertical system they are capable of forming; what interplay of correlation and dominance exists between them; what may be the effect of shifts, different temporalities, and various rehandlings; in what distinct totalities certain elements may figure simultaneously; in short, not only what series, but also what 'series of series' – or in other words, what 'tables' it is possible to draw up. A total description draws all phenomena around a single centre – a principle, a meaning, a spirit, a world-view, an overall shape; a general history, on the contrary would deploy the space of a dispersion.[33]

Fourth, the new history faces the problems of amassing 'coherent and homogeneous *corpora* of documents', establishing how one chooses and analyses relevances, defining the level of analysis, examining the formal structure that connects things, determining the groupings of distributions, geographic, periodic and so on. These problems have become part of the field of new history and can be contrasted to the problems of traditional history and above all its difficulty with the concept of development (*devenir*). Foucault contrasts these problems in terms of development (traditional history) and structure (new history), but suggests that the 'mutation' of history that has witnessed the emergence of the structural method of history is not complete. His point is that the significance and full implication of the relation between new history and the problems which it poses has not as yet been thought through clearly, and so the question becomes: why is it that this has not happened? Foucault's answer is both simple and profound:

> Continuous history is the indispensable correlative of the founding function of the subject: the guarantee that everything that has eluded him may be restored to him; the certainty that time will disperse nothing without restoring it in a reconstituted unity; the promise that one day the subject – that form of historical consciousness – will once again be able to appropriate, to bring back under his sway, all those things that are kept at a distance by difference, and find in them what might be called his abode.[34]

This dream of the function of the subject not only disallows the implications of the analysis of the operation of discontinuities and so on that has emerged out of the new history, but also resists any attempt at theoretical decentrings (Marx, Nietzsche, psychoanalysis, linguistics and ethnology) and is the foundation of two of the most familiar aspects of modern thought, 'the twin figures of anthropology and humanism'. Foucault suggests that, in the face of possible decentrings, continuous history is reactivated. Marx is made into a historian of totalities 'to rediscover in him the message of humanism'. Nietzsche is interpreted in terms of transcendental philosophy, and his genealogy is reduced 'to the level of a search for origins' and all the theoretical and philosophical problems brought into the open by new history are left 'to one side'. A consequence of this is that wherever the historian tries to pursue the elaboration of the categories of 'continuity and difference, threshold, rupture and transformation, and the description of series and limits', '[o]ne will be denounced for attacking the inalienable rights of history and the very foundations of any possible historicity'.[35]

Foucault suggests that a different form of history is now possible which is no longer dependent on the concept of development and its underlying principle of continuity, and that this eclipses traditional history and its provision of a secure home for continuous sovereign consciousness. His aim is not to introduce a structuralist method to the history of knowledge, although he acknowledges that his method and its results 'are not entirely foreign to what is called structural analysis'. It is to free his work from the 'anthropological theme' and humanism, so the work 'belongs to that field in which the questions of the human being, consciousness, origin, and the subject emerge, intersect, mingle and separate off'.[36]

This brings us back to the sentiment with which this chapter opened. Archaeology is profoundly connected with Foucault's analysis of the identity of the sovereign subject in our epoch. It attempts to fabricate a methodology that will be neither anthropological nor humanistic in an epoch dominated by anthropology and humanism. In this sense, *The Archaeology of Knowledge* is a retrospective definition of a methodology that emerged from work already undertaken in *Madness and Civilisation*, *The Birth of the Clinic* and *The Order of Things* and utilises the results of these works. It is an attempt to elaborate 'this blank space from which I speak, and which is slowly taking shape in a discourse that I still feel to be so precarious and unsure'.[37]

In the introduction to *The Archaeology of Knowledge*, we find as clear a statement as anywhere about how Foucault liked to conceive of his project, and its close association with the question of identity, and how it is fabricated. This cannot escape folding back on the subject that writes, speaks, lives and breathes, and in raising the question of the elaboration of identity one necessarily encounters a questioning of the production of one's own identity. How is it elaborated? How is it congealed? How are its points of coherence experienced, transformed and so on? How is it effaced?

It is as though in *The Archaeology of Knowledge* Foucault is attempting to analyse the discursive preconditions for the work he had already undertaken, and at the same time understand the condition of possibility for his own elaboration of himself as a subject. Perhaps there is a paradox here that is hard to unravel: is it possible to eclipse the hand that writes at the moment that it moves across the page? Is it possible to elide the anthropological and humanistic subject from the act that it operates on itself as it disappears? This possibility or impossibility diagrams the relative success or failure of *The Archaeology of Knowledge*.

The Archaeology of Knowledge takes up some of the theoretical problems posed by the new history – discontinuity, rupture, series – examining them in the context of the 'history of ideas, or of thought, or of science, or of knowledge'.[38] It does this by employing a number of strategies: first, in order to allow the problems of discontinuity to be effectively posed, everything that contributes to the theme of continuity in the history of ideas is evacuated from the study: tradition, evolution, development, influence, spirit and so on. Second, divisions between different discourses are put into question because these divisions are already the effects of 'reflexive categories, principles of classification, normative rules, institutionalised types'. Divisions such as the contemporary one between philosophy and literature have their own history as part of the ways in which statements are distributed, located and so on. They do not pre-exist this operation in some ideal way; rather, they are a consequence of it.

> In any case, these divisions – whether our own, or those contemporary with the discourse under examination – are always themselves reflexive categories, principles of classification, normative rules, institutionalized types: they, in turn, are facts of discourse that deserve to be analyzed beside others; of course, they also have complex relations with each other, but they are not intrinsically autochthonous, and universally recognizable characteristics.[39]

Third, the unity of the book and the *œuvre* is suspended.[40] Books are not unified objects in the sense that they are governed by the same principles of unity – books always refer among other things to other books, by the same author and other authors. This network of extended references is not the same for different kinds of works such as 'a mathematical treatise, a textual commentary, a historical account, and an episode in a novel cycle'. The ways in which a book is unified are different in each case, and once this is put into question it can be seen that the principles of unity of the book are already constructed 'on the basis of a complex field of discourse'.

The *œuvre* also poses a number of difficult problems. An *œuvre* is constituted by 'designating' a collection of texts to a proper name. This function of designation does not necessarily always operate in the same way – in this sense it is not unproblematically homogeneous. When one collects together an *œuvre*, the process of choosing what is in and what is out is problematic. Do you include all previous drafts and sketches; what about all the corrections and crossings-out; how does reported conversation fit into the picture? Do you include 'theoretical letters' and exclude scribbled notes written hastily to the children of friends? Do you include love letters, or letters to an accountant or a solicitor? What do you do about the salutations, greetings and messages on Christmas cards sent to friends?

The *œuvre* unproblematically presumes a deep level of unity that is in fact a function of commentary and other interpretive strategies, which overlay the fragments of a life's work with various unifying principles. It is these principles that bring the *œuvre* into being, attributing even the most insignificant details to 'the expression of the thought, the experience, the imagination, or the unconscious of the author, or, indeed, of the historical determinations that operated on him'.[41]

Finally, Foucault suggests that we must disconnect two opposite themes first:

> a wish that it should never be possible to assign, in the order of discourse, the irruption of a real event; that beyond any apparent beginning, there is always a secret origin – so secret and so fundamental that it can never be grasped in itself. Thus one is led inevitably, through the naïvety of chronologies, towards an ever-receding point that is never itself present in any history; this point is merely its own void; and from that point all beginnings can never be more than recommencements or occultation (in one and the same gesture, this *and* that).

and

> [that] all manifest discourse is secretly based on an 'already-said'; and that this 'already-said' is not merely a phrase that has already been spoken, or a text that has already been written, but a 'never-said', an incorporeal discourse, a voice as silent as a breath, a writing that is merely the hollow of its own mark. It is supposed therefore that everything that is formulated in discourse was already articulated in that semi-silence that precedes it, which continues to run obstinately beneath it, but which it covers and silences. The manifest discourse, therefore, is really no more than the repressive presence of what it does not say; and this 'not-said' is a hollow that undermines from within all that is said.[42]

The first theme directs historical analysis towards searching for and repeating an origin that ultimately 'eludes all historical determination', while the second sees historical analysis as interpreting the '"already-said" that is at the same time a "not-said"'. By contrast, what we need to do is hear the emergence of the sudden irruption of discourse as a specific and particular event. We need to consider each discourse to be a particularity relating to its own specific emergence as an event which enables it to be transformed, repeated and forgotten.

The point is not to reject all forms of continuity permanently, but to temporarily suspend the certain hold they have over us, to disturb the 'tranquillity with which they are accepted' and to show that they are the consequences of specific rules which can be analysed and questioned. In order to achieve this, you must examine the unities operating in a particular discursive field under analysis, such as medicine, political economy and so on, then interrogate the space which they claim is uniquely their own according to

> by what right they can claim a field that specifies them in space and a continuity that individualizes them in time; according to what laws they are formed; against the background of which discursive events they stand out; and whether they are not, in their accepted and quasi-institutional individuality, ultimately the surface effect of more firmly grounded unities.[43]

When the forces of all forms of continuity and series are suspended, it is possible then to undertake '*a pure description of discursive events*'. The discursive can be distinguished from 'language' because although the linguistic system is constructed from statements (discursive facts), 'a language is still a system for possible statements, a finite body of rules that authorizes an infinite number of performances'. In contrast to this, the field of discursive events is restricted to those 'linguistic sequences' that have already been formulated: while they may be vast in number they are nonetheless finite.

> The question posed by language analysis of some discursive fact or other is always: according to what rules has a particular state-ment been made, and consequently according to what rules could other similar statements be made? The description of the events of discourse poses a quite different question: how is it that one particular statement appeared rather than another?[44]

While this makes the distinction between language analysis and the analysis of discursive events, this point does not distinguish this methodology from the traditional methodology of the history of thought/history of ideas. So Foucault adds an important qualification:

that in contrast to the history of thought, the description of discursive events does not refer back beyond the event of the statement to the intention of the speaking subject: 'his conscious activity, what he meant, or, again, the unconscious activity that took place, despite himself, in what he said or in the almost imperceptible fracture of his actual words'.[45] In undertaking the analysis of the discursive event,

> We do not seek what is below what is manifest in the half silent murmur of another discourse; we must show why it could not be other than it was, in what respect it is exclusive of any other, how it assumes, in the midst of others and in relation to them, a place that no other could occupy. The question proper to such an analysis might be formulated in this way: what is this specific existence that emerges from what is said and nowhere else?[46]

Once the objective of *The Archaeology of Knowledge* is understood, the book itself is not so difficult to come to terms with as it might at first seem. It is constructed around issues that emerge directly out of the suspension of categories of unity, which leads Foucault to raise four problems framed by suspending the traditional unities and then posing other ways of analysing the relations between statements: first, in terms of the formation of a group that refers to the same object; second, whether they can be characterised as conforming to a certain style or manner; third, by 'determining the system of permanent and coherent concepts involved'; fourth, by grouping statements in terms of themes of analysis, for example evolution.[47] Foucault rejects each of his hypotheses and concludes:

> What one finds are rather various strategic possibilities that permit the activation of incompatible themes, again, the establishment of the same theme in different groups of statement. Hence the ideas of describing these dispersions themselves; of discovering whether, between these elements, which are certainly not organized as a progressively deductive structure, nor as an enormous book that is being gradually and continuously written, nor as the *œuvre* of a collective subject, one cannot discern a regularity: an order in their successive appearance, correlations in their simultaneity, assignable position in a common space, a reciprocal functioning, linked and hierarchized transformations. Such an analysis would not try to isolate small islands of coherence in order to describe their internal structure; it would not try to suspect and to reveal latent conflicts; it would study forms

of division. Or again: instead of reconstituting *chains of inference* (as one often does in the history of the sciences and philosophy), instead of drawing up *tables of differences* (as linguists do), it would describe *systems of dispersion*.[48]

The success or failure of *The Archaeology of Knowledge* is to be measured by each reader, and it would serve no purpose to summarise the entire book. The purpose of this discussion is to show that in spite of its focus on *discursive events* the underlying concern of *The Archaeology of Knowledge* is to continue Foucault's analysis of the role, function, construction and elaboration of the *subject*. In this sense, it is closely connected to, though quite different in its methodological practice from, *genealogy*.

> If we were to characterize it in two terms, then 'archaeology' would be the appropriate methodology of this analysis of local discursivities, and 'genealogy' would be the tactics whereby, on the basis of the descriptions of these local discursivities, the subjected knowledges which were thus released would be brought into play.[49]

Just as the question of identity introduced the work, so once again it is the question of identity that Foucault returns to at the end of *The Archaeology of Knowledge* having completed the study. The Conclusion continues the discussion between Foucault and the imaginary interlocutor which commenced the Introduction and takes the form of an interrogation of his objectives for the book and an evaluation of its success. He suggests that the crux of the difference between his work and that of others is revealed by the imaginary question: is it history or philosophy? He responds that while his work is part of a decentring that leaves no privileged centre of any kind, it does not do this by finding in discourse 'in the depths of things said, at the very place in which they are silent, the moment of their birth (whether this is seen as their empirical creation, or the transcendental act that gives them origin); it does not set out to be a recollection of the original or a memory of the truth'.[50] There are a number of important issues to be drawn out here; first, the attitude of the researcher to the work at hand. The researcher does not simply do their work and discover a pre-existing knowledge through the competency of the application of their research method. Second, the researcher cannot find beneath the clamour of discourse the moment of the creative articulation in the existence of a subject that exceeds it. In this sense, it is not a

re-creative act. Third, it does not involve correspondence to a transcendental truth of things.

> On the contrary, its task is to *make* differences: to constitute
> them as objects, to analyse them, and to define their concept.
> Instead of travelling over the field of discourses in order to
> recreate the suspended totalizations for its own use, instead of
> seeking in what has been said that *other* hidden discourse, which
> nevertheless remains the *same* (and instead of playing endlessly
> with *allegory* and *tautology*), it is continually making *differentia-*
> *tions*, it is a *diagnosis*. If philosophy is memory or a return of the
> origin, what I am doing cannot, in any way, be regarded as
> philosophy; and if the history of thought consists in giving life
> to half-effaced figures, what I am doing is not history either.[51]

Foucault's imaginary critic then attacks him for making claims
about archaeology in terms of what 'intentions' and 'hopes' he had
for it, claiming that Foucault demands for himself a creative role that
his work has excluded for others:

> Have you not deprived individuals of the right to intervene per-
> sonally in the positivities in which their discourses are situated?
> You have linked their slightest words to obligations that condemn
> their slightest innovations to conformity. You make revolution
> very easy for yourself, but very difficult for others. It might be
> better if you had a clearer awareness of the conditions in which
> you speak, and a greater confidence in the real action of men
> and in their possibilities.[52]

Foucault's response is illuminating in terms of the overall direction
of his work, and draws this chapter back to where it began. He
replies that when a critic poses the question to him in this way, they
make certain assumptions about freedom and the subject. This is to
assert that a consciousness transparent to itself lies underneath
transformations in discursive practice, and this brings on the scene
both a political and a theoretical problem.

He reiterates his view that to speak

> is to do something – something other than to express what one
> thinks; to translate what one knows, and sometimes other than
> to play with the structures of a language (*langue*); to show that
> to add a statement to a pre-existing series of statements is to
> perform a complicated and costly gesture, which involves

conditions (and not only a situation, a context, and motives), and rules (not the logical and linguistic rules of construction); to show that a change in the order of discourse does not presuppose 'new ideas', a little invention and creativity, a different mentality, but transformations in a practice, perhaps also in neighbouring practices, and in their common articulation. I have not denied – far from it – the possibility of changing discourse: I have deprived the sovereignty of the subject of the exclusive and instantaneous right to it.[53]

and

Has not the practice of revolutionary discourse and scientific discourse in Europe over the past two hundred years freed you from this idea that words are wind, an external whisper, a beating of the wings that one has difficulty in hearing in the serious matter of history? Or must we conclude that in order to refuse this lesson, you are determined to misunderstand discursive practices, in their own existence, and that you wished to maintain in spite of that lesson, a history of the mind, of rational knowledge, ideas, and opinions? What is that fear which makes you reply in terms of consciousness when someone talks to you about a practice, its conditions, its rules, and its historical transformations? What is that fear which makes you seek, beyond all boundaries, ruptures, shifts, and divisions, the great historico-transcendental destiny of the Occident?[54]

Foucault suggests that this 'fear' emerges from a haunting impression unable to recognise that consciousness does not exceed its specific and particular emergence in the event of its own momentary appearance.

Must we admit that the time of discourse is not the time of consciousness extrapolated to the dimensions of history, or the time of history present in the form of consciousness?
   ... They cannot bear (and one cannot but sympathize) to hear someone saying: 'Discourse is not life: its time is not your time; in it, you will not be reconciled to death; you may have killed God beneath the weight of all that you have said; but don't imagine that, with all that you are saying, you will make a man that will live longer than he'.[55]

The Order of Things and *The Archaeology of Knowledge* both conclude with the theme of the disappearance of 'man' – as a discrete object of knowledge and a transcending originating consciousness. They illustrate how the implications of questions posed by these interrelated themes, first raised in the nineteenth century, have come to occupy a critical space within the formation of knowledge today – a space stretched between the concepts continuity, identity and subject(ion), which demands that they be addressed in a thoughtful way. *The Order of Things* and *The Archaeology of Knowledge* constitute elements of this thoughtful address, and their value is perhaps less to be measured in terms of the answers that they offer but rather more in terms of their success in placing the importance of the interrogation on the agenda.

> What realm do we enter which is neither the history of knowledge, nor history itself; which is controlled by neither the teleology of truth nor the rational sequence of causes, since causes have value and meaning only beyond the division? A realm no doubt, where what is in question is the limits rather than the identity of a culture.[56]

NOTES

1. Foucault, op. cit., *The Archaeology of Knowledge*, p. 17.
2. See Chapters 1 and 4.
3. Foucault, op. cit., *Politics Philosophy Culture*, 'On Power', p. 99.
4. Foucault., op. cit., *The Order of Things*, p. xiv.
5. See Barker, op. cit., pp. 47–8.
6. For more on continuity/discontinuity, see Chapter 1.
7. Foucault, op. cit., *Power/Knowledge*, 'Truth and Power', p. 114.
8. This connects closely with Foucault's account of truth and history: see Chapters 1 and 2.
9. Foucault, op. cit., *Power/Knowledge*, 'Truth and Power', p. 131.
10. Foucault, op. cit., *The Order of Things*, p. xi.
11. Ibid., p. xiv.
12. Foucault, op. cit., *The Archaeology of Knowledge*: 'It is an attempt to define a particular site by the exteriority of its vicinity; rather than by trying to reduce others to silence, by claiming that what they say is worthless . . .', p. 17.
13. Ibid., pp. 21–5.
14. Ibid., p. 23.
15. Ibid., p. 169.
16. Ibid., p. 170.
17. Ibid., pp. 181–2.
18. Foucault, op. cit., *The Order of Things*, p. xxii.
19. Ibid., p. 168.
20. Foucault, op. cit., *Power/Knowledge*, 'Confessions of the Flesh', pp. 196–7.
21. Ibid., p. 197.

22. Burchell et al., op. cit., *The Foucault Effect*, Foucault, 'Politics and the Study of Discourse', p. 55.
23. Foucault, op. cit., *The Order of Things*, p. 387.
24. For more on this, see Chapter 4.
25. Foucault, op. cit., *The Archaeology of Knowledge*, back cover.
26. Ibid., p. 3.
27. Ibid., pp. 3–4.
28. Ibid., pp. 5–6.
29. Ibid., p. 6.
30. Ibid., pp. 6–7.
31. Ibid., p. 7.
32. Ibid., p. 9.
33. Ibid., p. 10.
34. Ibid., p. 12.
35. Ibid., p. 14.
36. Ibid., p. 16.
37. Ibid., p. 17.
38. Ibid., p. 21.
39. Ibid., p. 22.
40. For more on this, see Chapter 1.
41. Foucault, op. cit., *The Archaeology of Knowledge*, p. 24. Refer to Chapter 1 of this book, 'Body and Text'.
42. Foucault, op. cit., *The Archaeology of Knowledge*, p. 25.
43. Ibid., p. 26.
44. Ibid., p. 27.
45. Ibid.
46. Ibid., p. 28.
47. Ibid., pp. 33–5.
48. Ibid., p. 37.
49. Foucault, op. cit., *Power/Knowledge*, 'Two Lectures', p. 85.
50. Foucault, op. cit., *The Archaeology of Knowledge*, p. 205.
51. Ibid., pp. 205–6.
52. Ibid., p. 208.
53. Ibid., p. 209.
54. Ibid., pp. 209–10.
55. Ibid., pp. 210–11.
56. Foucault, op. cit., *Madness and Civilisation*, p. xi.

6

THINKING AGAINST FOUCAULT[1]

In the Introduction to this book, the possibility of establishing a critical relation to the work of Foucault that was not reductive, and that multiplied the meanings and interpretations of his work, was theorised. From this point, the attempt was undertaken to present an analysis that would not be a commentary, but would serve as an expansive repetition of Foucault's work that would direct the reader back to the primary sources.

With this in mind, I would like to return to the problem of how it is possible to present a productive yet critical interaction with the work of Foucault (or indeed anyone else), and in order to elaborate this further I want to explore two kinds of reading of Foucault that help to draw out possible differences in the kinds of critical interaction with a body of work.

In the first case, a 'negative' reading of Foucault is presented that is one of closure and reduction. It employs an attitude and tone which suggests a profound antipathy at having the foundations of the reader's own thought challenged.[2] Rather than using this antipathy productively, in the sense of producing something different, the reader develops their arguments not only to dismiss any positive benefits that may come from an encounter with Foucault, but to ward off those who might be seduced into taking on this work productively. This becomes part of a wider project, insofar as Foucault is transformed into a metaphorical figure for a 'particular' kind of continental thinking and becomes 'a central figure in a disgraceful metamorphosis of continental philosophy':

> For these post-philosophical philosophers mock at the claims of all knowledge, but are little prone to extend scepticism to their own comprehensive negative views on science and society. Refusing all critical debate, they seem to labour on the illusion

that the absence of method and the neglect of argumentative rigour leads automatically to a virtuous grasp of 'real problems'. They do not blush to pass as writers rather than professional thinkers, yet the 'literary' cloak barely covers a huge dogmaticism.[3]

What is to be done with a statement such as this? Should one be drawn into making the appropriate corrections, defending Foucault in his absence? Should I allow myself to occupy this absence and momentarily sketch lines of resistance? Where does Foucault speak of science in the sense of pure sciences? Does he not always confine himself to the human sciences? Why does is this ignored? Does Foucault not refer to himself as an optimist – a happy positivist? Why is this forgotten? Is not Foucault endlessly engaged in a critical debate with those who do not always agree with him: Sartre, Althusser, Derrida, Deleuze, Chomsky, Habermas, Braudel, Lacan and so on? Why is this not mentioned? Is Foucault not argumentatively rigorous in his books? Why is no apparent awareness of the necessary differences in argumentative style between the written pieces and the conversational ones exhibited? Does Foucault expressly refer not to the 'Real' but only to the real? Is it not this that leads to his nominalism and a profound anti-dogmatism? Why is this not acknowledged?

At last it appears that a critical encounter with this 'negative' reading of Foucault is starting to take shape. Foucault is the best of everything: more logical than the logical positivists, more realist than Lovejoy and Whitehead, more materialist than Armstrong, more idealist than Plato and Collingwood. But now I see clearly the double trap that has been set and how naïvely I have tumbled into it. First, by uncritically putting forward the claim that Foucault's critics from within a particular body of thought are just mistaken, or have not read him carefully enough, I have been drawn into accepting the pre-eminence of a certain philosophical paradigm, and more particularly a style of thinking, and have forced Foucault into it.

Second, in doing this I have asserted my mastery over his work not to expand my own thought but in order to limit it and therefore the possibilities for my own self-elaboration. I have disciplined and subjected myself within what is sometimes referred to as 'the Anglo-American theoretical paradigm'. If this double trap is to be avoided, then what other possible reactions to this style of criticism can be mustered?[4]

In the first place, it seems that this 'negative' reading of Foucault assumes that there is a realm of 'non-post-philosophy' philosophy – a realm where 'Philosophy' is still practised, where critical debate is engaged in, method is prioritised, argument and rigour abound, real problems are dealt with and professional thinkers do their work in a non-dogmatic atmosphere.[5]

Rather than simply suggesting that this is what Foucault does anyway, the implications of this can be rethought in terms of where such a realm might be found and how it might function, and we can postulate that it might be located in the geo-philosophical domain mostly dominated by Anglo-American philosophy departments.[6]

This immediately raises important issues that revolve around the question of geo-philosophy. In particular, it refers to the much-repeated but rarely defined distinction between Continental thought and Anglo-American thought which operates in many different disciplinary regimes, but especially in Philosophy and is often little more than an association with a list of proper names. On the one hand, Marx, Freud, Nietzsche, Heidegger, Sartre, Foucault, Irigaray, Deleuze, Derrida, Kristeva – and on the other, Mill, Hobbes, Locke, Hume, Russell, Wittgenstein, Fraser, Rorty, Chomsky, Austin and so on. However, it is clearly not enough simply to associate a proper name unproblematically with each of the series. In the first instance, who occupies a position in either camp is extremely fluid, and in the second, there are names who have their theoretical 'feet' in both camps: Spinoza, Leibniz, Descartes, Locke, Plato, Rousseau, Kant, Hegel, Hobbes, Rorty, Hume, Hacking and so on. So, if it is not so much a question of drawing out the philosophical content of a series of proper names – what is the basis of this distinction?

WHAT IS PHILOSOPHY?

This question What is Philosophy? has a long tradition within the history of philosophy. What is taken for theology in one age is taken to be philosophy in another.[7] What is taken for science in one age is seen as philosophy in another. The thought content of philosophy has always been fluid and in part resolved according to the politics of theory, rather than the relative merit or otherwise of a particular position. If, for the moment, we take the 'politics of theory' out of the picture, we are left with, in terms of the attributable characteristics of philosophy, critical debate, prioritised method, argument and rigour, real problems, professional thinking and non-dogmaticism. However, as I suggested earlier, these features alone are not enough to allow us to make a clear distinction between Anglo-American philosophy and the work of Foucault.

Therefore, this difference cannot be simply ascribed either to a set of methodological principles such as those referred to above, or to which 'particular' names appear in a prescribed canon. Perhaps this difference, then, is more to do with a particular style of thinking – a style of thinking that involves a specific relation to something that can be described as *the*, not a, subject. In Chapter 4, the double sense in which Foucault uses the word 'subject' was analysed in some detail. To this a third meaning can now be added, a subject in the sense of an 'academic' discipline.[8] This triple play becomes: subject as an 'academic' discipline, subject as subjected/disciplined identity, subject as that which subjects. In this first sense, the subject of Anglo-American philosophy in our contemporary epoch is surely constituted by reference to its central thematic the *Cogito*.

With the exception of 'professional thinking', the principles of philosophy – such as critical debate, prioritised method, argument and rigour, real problems, non-dogmaticism – could be taken straight from the *Discourse on Method*.[9] The issue of 'professional' thinking will be taken up later, but for the moment we might consider that the contemporary consequence of the work of Descartes is precisely what is most at issue in the work not only of Foucault but also of many of his contemporaries.[10] There is more than a little irony in the fact that the apparent 'grounding' subject of both 'non-philosophical philosophy' and Anglo-American philosophy is Descartes, and the difference between them is to be found less in their method or object and more in their relation to their respective subjects.[11]

For Foucault, the Cartesian subject, wherever it is found, and its many consequences are precisely what need to be put into question, to be problematised, to be interrogated in order to 'destruct' the reductive foundationalism to which it leads. For some of those who criticise him, 'thinking' is not possible without continuous foundations, be they methodological or historical. In the first instance, thought must be reduced to its foundations, to itself, before philosophical work can be undertaken. But how is it possible to reduce thought to itself – to a pure abstraction of its own method? Is this not another version of attempting to reach a philosophical real, where thought and thinking are reduced to one? Would not such a practical technology have to exclude and then excommunicate all that it does not recognise as itself? So perhaps in part, what is at stake here are disciplinary relations tied to the emergence and sustaining of 'professional thinking' (only possible after the emergence of the professional philosopher/academic).

This takes us directly to the question of the politics of theory, which is part of a theoretical transformation – made possible by Kant and revitalised by Heidegger – that is still under way, and which investigates not the problems of philosophy as such, but the problem of *thinking*. The question What is Philosophy? is now paralleled and informed by another, What is Thinking?, and both are drawn out by the politics of theory.

THE POLITICS OF THEORY

It would be possible to undertake a history of the emergence of philosophy as a discipline. Perhaps one might begin with an account of the medieval recovery of Greek texts, then move on to scholasticism, rationalism, empiricism and so on. One would eventually arrive in the eighteenth century and chart the emergence of philosophy as a discrete discipline within the university. One would see it consolidated during the nineteenth century, attempt to take on the mantle of the scientific and then trace it up to our present age.

No doubt a good deal of interesting 'positivist' work could be undertaken. One could trace the number of chairs of philosophy at universities – perhaps even the number of lecturers and more recently students; one might examine the courses given, the references used. One could plot curves, analyse what was taught where, what comprised the canon. One could look at how philosophy interacted with other disciplines such as history, anthropology, literary studies, the social sciences, and more recently cultural studies and so on. Such a labour could take a lifetime; and, just as it showed many things, so in all probability it would also cover up many others: the petty jealousies, the never-ending struggle for one theoretical position to dominate and silence another. The impossible theoretical choices made, the strategies set to seduce students, and to attract funding, the paternalism, the patronage, the cultural imperialism, the disciplinary strategies, and the secret handshakes imposed on those who would join the 'academic' club. What would remain hidden would be something that we can term the politics of theory within a particular discipline in the university.[12] But once again we find ourselves standing astride a doubly dangerous abyss.

This takes two related forms: first the distinction between the university and the outside, and second the function of the university.

The university 'usually' goes to some length to distinguish itself from the outside – from an everyday existence that is not a university experience. It establishes this by practical differentiations: arrival and departure times, academic sabbaticals, continuous examinations, and also by what it takes to be its function and objective: the pursuit of learning in an atmosphere of mutual cooperation. However, what enables much of this to operate is the construction of something that is not exactly a private space but is not exactly a public space either, and although this exchange is always a fluid one, it is important that an imaginary but nonetheless real demarcation between academic space and public space be maintained.[13]

But is it possible to think about this 'differently' in terms of what it is that happens in this carefully constructed academic space, by considering the issue of what function it serves. Foucault suggests that the university has two functions: first, to put young people between the ages of 18 and 25 out of circulation, and second, to constitute a normalising basis which will allow them to be integrated 'peacefully' into society at large when their studies have ended:

> Finally, the student is given a gamelike way of life; he is offered a kind of distraction, amusement, freedom which, again, has nothing to do with real life; it is this kind of artificial, theatrical society, a society of cardboard, that is being built around him; and thanks to this, young people from 18–25 are thus, as it were, neutralized by and for society, rendered safe, ineffective, socially and politically castrated. There is the first function of the university: to put students out of circulation. Its second function, however, is one of integration. Once a student has spent six or seven years of his life within this artificial society, he becomes 'absorbable': society can consume him. Insidiously, he will have received the values of this society. He will have been given socially desirable modes of behaviour, so that this ritual of exclusion will finally take on the value of inclusion and recuperation or reabsorption.[14]

This reabsorption takes one of two forms, either reabsorption into society at large, or continuing endless reabsorption as an academic within the university system itself. There, academics themselves increasingly face constant examination of their work both internally and externally to their own institution, and struggle to maintain their own interests in their teaching programme while still undertaking continuing 'high-quality' research. Under the continuing pressure of the bureaucratising of the universities though funding regimes, research grants – and in some cases the imposition of Total Quality Management and Quality Assurance strategies – the administration of the university disciplines its academics as well as its students. To be an academic today is to be both disciplined and a disciplinarian.[15]

Of course, there is always a danger of rogue undisciplined moments – the writer/thinker who does not care much either for personal appropriation or for claiming for themself the illusory objective serenity of ivy-covered colleges. It was thinkers like Freud, Nietzsche and Marx writing/thinking outside the university who reinaugurated the beginning of a theoretical decentring of both subject, and subject as discipline. It is here that we find the emergence of a decentring critical discourse that, while it takes on many of the methodological principles of its objects, nonetheless attempts to pull away their foundations from under them.

It is this that many of Foucault's 'negative' critics are responding to, from the basis that we can have our intellectual disagreements as often and as intensively as we like as long as in our theoretical practice we agree to defend certain fundamental principles that assure the sanctity of our method and the subject underpinning it. This is what cannot be called into question, otherwise the possibility emerges that the whole project of disciplinary subjection as 'we define it' will fall apart. Most critically, the 'we' who determine this are the 'we' of a particular authorised and dominant cadre within a university community.

At the beginning of this chapter, I suggested that different kinds of critical interaction are possible with a body of work. In contrast to the limited and limiting 'negative' critical response which I have outlined above, I want seriously to consider the possibility of developing a more productive style of critical interaction, that we might think of in the more interactive terminology of *thinking against*.

THINKING AGAINST

What is thinking against? Thinking against is a form of critical interaction that involves touching the work of the other. This is a meeting of surfaces: to be against is to be touching, so this critical encounter is not a reading, not a seeing, but a feeling, a touching difference. In the interplay of surfaces against each other, new lines of attachment are made, new forms of experience take shape. To think against is to expand and multiply possible encounters – to

think against is to seriously take on the concept of 'agonism'.[16]
What are some of the features of *thinking against*?

1. To think against is always to think against the present. Whatever its precise form, be it historical, scientific or otherwise, it takes the present as its object. In this sense, it is an attempt to find a way out of the present.

2. To think against involves touching a body of work, a corpus, and so it is profoundly materialist.[17]

3. To think against is to problematise, while at the same time historicising the context of a problem to be analysed.

4. To think against is to draw diagrams for the construction and experience of particular forms of subject/subjection.

5. To think against is to follow unexpected changes of direction and not exclude them from what is finally produced. It is to allow chance connections, surprising lines of association to disrupt the more disciplined aspects of a totalising theoretical elaboration.

6. To think against is to think against the exclusivity of developmental and progressive notions of theoretical elaboration.

7. To think against is to take the object of thought seriously while at the same time not without humour.

8. To think against is to think in the model of thought as music. Many parts to one score, many progressions, digressions, modulations and transformations. Many tones, many entries and exits. Theory and practice are joined in the production of a sound experience – even discords, with a sometimes delicate touch producing harmonic multiples that not everyone can always hear.

9. To think against is to illustrate the particular material specificity of thought.

10. To think against is always to emphasise the surfaces of things. This does not mean that they are at the same level but that every level can be only the surface of another surface.

11. To think against is to analyse the level of a surface, not to get closer to or further from the truth or objective reality but to reveal other surfaces and points of contact.

12. To think against is to return to a thought only to redistribute its differences and diagram alternative identities.

13. To think against is to understand that thought is both a material practice and a figure at the same time. It is wholly

figurative. In thinking, a figuring-out happens – surfaces emerge, foci change.

14. Thinking against exists only in the realm of positivities – and serves to disrupt all reductions.

15. Thinking against shows up some of the subtleties of the politics of theory and the insidious and persistent virility of certain kinds of thinking. It involves diagnosis where diagnostics are made against the body of the other and involve touching/feeling and surface encounters.[18]

There are a number of examples of thinking against, including Foucault's own work in relation to Roussel, Blanchot, Sade, Bataille, Artaud, Marx and Nietzsche, but perhaps it is harder to find a better example than Deleuze's book on Foucault.[19] However, for a shorter and more compressed example of thinking against, I want to re-present work undertaken to mark the tenth anniversary of Foucault's death.

FOUCAULT'S SUBLIME: THINKING AGAINST FOUCAULT AND LONGINUS[20]

It is always difficult to trace beginnings, as such a tracing requires a figure already there which mediates between beginning and end. Reflecting on the absence of both, by chance I found a translation of Longinus' letter known as *On Elevation of Style* or *The Sublime*. What initially attracted my attention was that it was a peculiarly Australian event. Translated by T. G. Tucker, Professor Emeritus of Classical Philology at the University of Melbourne, it was printed in Australia and published by Melbourne University Press in 1935 – a message from the colonies to an Empire in decline and introduced by a profound index of its placement: 'In a gold-mining country one may perhaps be excused for putting it that "the Longinus claim" keeps on crushing nearly twenty hundredweight to the ton'.[21] It was the irony that claimed me and led to my astonishment: a communication from the mining colonies to the Empire claiming the high ground on the *Elevation of Style*, with a mining analogy in a text which like the mine is one of bits and pieces, spaces and odd remnants.

Unfortunately, the sublime has for the most part not managed to recover from the ravages of the Enlightenment, when it was set into opposition with itself and from which it has still not yet been able to completely take flight, and from the fact that in the eighteenth century Romanticism found expression in the misleading dichotomy of the sublime and the beautiful.[22]

The Enlightenment had mistaken a misanthropic solitary asceticism for a dialectic of the sublime, and, in order to give force to the beautiful, its antithesis, the sublime was reduced to being the ugly, shadowy counterpart of the beautiful. This event allows us to pose the question that if the history of the Enlightenment has been marked by this opposition, is it possible to re-present the sublime as an active force? And further, on what basis could such an activity be generated? To return to Longinus:

> For the effect of superlative passages is not merely to persuade the hearer, but to carry him off his feet. The cogent or the pleasing must always give way to the startling effect of the wonderful. Whereas it generally lies with ourselves to be persuaded or not, the fine passages in question carry with them such an irresistible force and mastery as to overpower any hearer. Moreover, skilful argument and a deft arrangement and handling of our materials are not made apparent by one or two sentences, but must reveal themselves gradually from the whole texture of a speech, whereas a splendid utterance, produced at the proper moment, comes like a thunderbolt, pulverises all mere facts, and displays the full power of the speaker in a single flash.[23]

Here we have delineated the constitutive features of the sublime – elevation, revelation, a proper moment, a thunderbolt – a single flash. All this carries one away – to new heights. Demosthenes is the archetypal transmitter of the sublime who is compared by Longinus to 'a lightning stroke or thunderbolt for the vehemence, rapidity, energy, and terrific effect with which he both fires and shatters',[24] and again:

> I say, because he absorbed all these potent gifts – which are apparently god-sent, for one dare not call them human – he surpasses any and every speaker by the virtues which he possesses, while dispensing with those which he does not possess, and so overcomes by his thunder and lightning all the orators of all time. It would be easier to confront a rushing thunderbolt with open eye than to face his rapid flashes of passion.[25]

This sublime is almost irresistible, but is a wholly active productive experience, an enlightening blinding flash. And yet what is it about this sublime of Longinus that would allow us to distance it from that of the Enlightenment? As Longinus tells us:

With the practical argument the orator has combined a vivid presentation, and has, by the joint effect, gone further than mere logical persuasion could go. In such cases we always instinctively obey the stronger call, and for that reason we are forcibly diverted from that which merely demonstrates to that which carries us off our feet with its vividness, whereby the literal argument is buried in a blaze of light. That experience is not surprising; for, when two forces are brought into line with each other, the more potent always absorbs the virtue of the other.[26]

This is a sublime that by virtue of its brilliance absorbs both the rational and the dialectical in the single line of its own release of energy. The brilliance of the sublime is that it creates multiple transparencies or, at worst, translucencies, because darkness is inimical to the sublime.

Longinus suggests that there are five 'fountainheads' of the sublime which rest on the command of language 'without which we can do nothing':

1. a capacious grasp of thoughts and ideas;
2. strong and vehement passion;
3. the construction of figures (which are of two kinds, one consisting in the turn of thought, the other in the turn of expression);[27]
4. admirable diction (of which, again, the parts are the choice of words and the coining of imaginative turns)
5. serving as a frame compacting all the rest, a masterly structural arrangement.

According to Longinus, the first two – a capacious grasp of thoughts and ideas and strong and vehement passion – are natural capacities; the last three are techniques that can be learned. Longinus suggests that the combination of a capacious grasp of vehement passion and thoughts and ideas is to be found when a conception covers a great distance from heaven to earth, amplifies the extraordinary, astonishes and startles. Such a conception is as magnificent and unpredictable as thunderbolts and lightning themselves, and this brings together elevation, height and motion under the sign of the sublime.

Longinus goes to some lengths to detail the parameters of these conceptions for his contemporaries, but for us this is an impossible return. What remains is just the lightning flash, the thunderbolt, and the possibility of abjuring dialectics which allows a provisional redrawing of a figure of the Enlightenment and its carefully constructed double problematics – sublime/beauty, rational/irrational – without being for or against it.[28] In this way, we can address the question 'what is it today?' that restores to us a wholly active non-dialectical moment of the sublime, which Foucault has discussed variously as attraction (Blanchot), desire (Sade), force (Nietzsche), transgression (Bataille), materiality of thought (Artaud): collectively <thought from the outside>.[29]

This becomes an analytic counter-restoration that elevates precisely at that moment when all that is recognisably human disappears, because it is bathed in a brilliance and energy so intense that the ground is cleared around it.[30] The intensity of the sublime always involves relative distance: close/far, bright/dull, descent/ascent, not as oppositions but as magnifications, amplifications and modulations, because proximity is constitutive of the possibility of any specific determination.[31] This includes proximity to the production of oneself as a subject that is subjected in the knowledge of one's own material finitude[32] – an astonishing moment that comes from the clearing around the finitude of one's being, death.

Has anyone ever existed who was not aware of the finite materiality of their own existence? Is this not the general problematic and condition of 'human' existence? Nowadays this often amounts to refusing to transform an age-old question – why must we die? – to a new profoundly nominal question. What is the effect of the problematic of finitude on our everyday existence? Further to this, and more amazing: does a language yet exist that will allow us to engage with this problematic? This is the line on which Foucault's thought from the outside transfigures the work of Artaud, Blanchot, Nietzsche, Sade and Bataille and draws out the impossible limit of our finitude.

Will the event of death take place with greater speed than it can be formulated within language? Will we dissolve into the outside faster than we can articulate the experience of its arrival or disappearance? This 'unrepresentable' of language, this limit, then returns as a critique of the possibility of any complete, essential universal system of representation.[33]

This is what draws transgression beyond its own limits, to a language not yet heard but which already exists – a drawing that lies in wait for its figuring out, its transfiguration. Neither beautiful nor ugly, just sublime. But if this moment of capture is not essential, on what does it rest? Perhaps it rests on the provisional – on uncertain repetitions – coincidental flights? The same coincidence that put that foxy-madness into [Fou](fuchs)cault's name. But is this not far too cerebral, privileging imagining over material existence – another idealism – another Platonism? Another dialectic?

Perhaps the proper respect can only be given to these questions by not attempting to answer them just now and instead to reconfigure the already said. The moment of the sublime, of the disappearance of the unified self, is bound by the materiality of the finitude of physical existence. A moment that is sublime precisely because it is configured within the experience of finitude. Lightning requires of the clearing that it surround the space of the flash – the clearing elevates itself at the moment the lightning earths. It is our limited materiality that draws into being the 'immaterial', our finite existence that allows us to elevate ourselves to the infinite.[34]

But if lightning and distance are constitutive of the sublime, we must not forget passion, the second of Longinus' natural elements. It is the possibility of passion that allows us an active living engagement with the sublime – with its eroticism, its brilliance, its passionate dangers bordered by the dazzling revelations that accompany the thrilling terror of looking directly at a brilliant light[35] – of looking directly into the sun. A passion that disperses and multiplies is a passion that draws the sublime, a draught of the future that is an implicit critique of Plato's poisonous potion and always threatens its own violent Annunciation. Every possible dispersal conjures up this sublime possibility, insofar as we are aggregates of materials and forces; to multiply the possibilities of the exchange is to encounter the limit – the outside. Cell to cell, synaptic flash with synaptic flash, fold with fold. This limit is also the encounter of the limit, in the clearing of the sublime. Perhaps, as Foucault suggests,

> Transgression carries the limit right to the limit of its being; transgression forces the limit to the fact of its imminent disappearance, to find itself in what it excludes (perhaps, to be more exact, to recognize itself for the first time), to experience its positive truth in its downward fall? And yet, toward what is transgression unleashed in its movement of pure violence, if not that which imprisons it, toward the limit and those elements it contains? What bears the brunt of its aggression and to what void does it owe the unrestrained fullness of its being, if not that which it crosses in its violent act and which, as its destiny, it crosses out the line it effaces?[36]

This is also the limit of the language of our own materiality; it is the foundational relation we have with ourselves, the inside of the curve or the fold. This is both the separation and the unity of the inside and the outside and is a relation that is inscribed within Foucault's third aspect of the struggle of the subject: 'that which ties the individual to himself and submits him to others . . .'.[37] This moment has revealed itself (again?) in our epoch and presents a diagram of an ethics of the self which flashes into light – particle and wave – sketching a transformed aes-thetics. An aesthetics that is neither Greek, nor Romantic European, nor the uniform trajectory of one to the other, but that turns on the *thetic* which is characterised as *laying down or setting forth; involving* [only] *positive statement*.

This necessarily leads to Foucault's *limit attitude* which involves 'a critique of what we are saying, thinking, and doing, through a historical ontology of ourselves'.[38] This limit attitude places thought at the frontier of its own limit – abandoning the search for the discovery of continuously repeated universal structures and instead focusing on how it is that we have come to recognise ourselves as the subjects which we recognise ourselves to be. In attending to this task, we must necessarily transgress the limits of our being in history, which in turn announces another historical event that effects and requires another modulation of ourselves. This is, as Foucault suggests, 'the undefined work of freedom'.[39]

But why does this require an encounter with a diagram of the sublime? Perhaps it is because at this time in our possible existences we encounter the experience that at some time in the foreseeable future the thought of the sublime may no longer exist.

There was a time when it was conceivable that the Gods would no longer inhabit our world, there was a time when it was conceivable that God had died. Now we live in an age of conceiving of the death of the entire species, even of all life-forms on the planet. This presents the possibility to us that the sublime may no longer be thought, the outside might trace the inside, every fold might be pulled into a straight line. Death may no longer be the clearing but be all there is, and the passionate embrace of the sublime may dissolve into an empty lifeless landscape with everything reduced to the inanimate. Lifeless objects orbiting through the space of the real, encountering multiple lifeless substrata. A point of absolute irreducibility. Of absolute presence.

Yet what is so astonishing in this vision is not its cataclysmic millenarian pessimism but its appalling anthropomorphism, and its naïve attempt to imply that the existence of anything meaningful is dependent upon human reflection of the sublime. Does the sublime demand of itself that it be recognised, or is it rather that today humanity demands of itself that it recognise its unique dependence on the problematic of the sublime? In other words, *today*, encounters with the sublime are profound encounters with ourselves.[40]

This surely is the return of Foucault, whose work constantly forces us to encounter ourselves in the production of knowledge about ourselves. An inescapable return, an inescapable encounter which does not have to be endured but can be worked upon as we work upon ourselves by embracing an ethical, *thetic* dimension. A passionate dangerous dimension that embraces the sublime in the production of thunderbolts and lightning and for that instant temporarily defers the slippage of outside and inside.

This is the conjunction of a line of flight of Longinus and Foucault. Their work is itself sublime as it storms, rails, thunders and now and again strikes the ground with a brilliant and enlightening flash. But today there are no Gods to encounter, today the encounter is with ourselves, in our finitude, and in the knowledge that we are constructed as what we are as an effect of power/knowledge relations circulating within analysable practices and regimes. It is here that we meet Foucault's insistence that we question this moment in our epoch with rigour and an irritating persistence that may create an opening for ourselves. As Foucault suggests, referring to Raymond Roussel:

> It is true that the first text one writes is neither written for others, nor for who one is: one writes to become someone other than who one is. Finally there is an attempt at modifying one's way of being through the act of writing. It is this transformation of his way of being that he observed, he believed in, he sought after, and for which he suffered horribly.[41]

In the already said of Foucault, we can encounter ourselves as new surfaces, new folds, new lines and new meanings. In these encounters, we have the opportunity of reaching out to the sublime as we also engage in a flight from ourselves and from everything that we have become. Then our epitaph and Foucault's momentarily fuse in the line of reciprocal line of flight from oneself, most beautifully drawn out by Nietzsche: those

> who are impatient and gloomily inclined towards themselves and in all they do resemble rampaging horses, and who derive from their own works, indeed, only a shortlived fire and joy

which almost bursts their veins and then a desolation and sourness made more wintry by the contrasts it presents – how
should such men endure to remain within *themselves*! They long
to dissolve into something *'outside'* . . .[42]

To come back to the beginning of this chapter. Is it useful to think
of the major lines of critical thought in respect of the work of
Foucault in terms of thinking against? Is it helpful to frame this work
with the question *to what extent do his major critics engage in thinking
against him*, in the way that I have been attempting to outline? Should
we value critical work by asking the question *to what extent does it
avoid being too reductive in relation to its subject/object interaction, but
rather uses a critical encounter to multiply the possibilities of thought*? Or
to put this a rather more Foucauldian way, to what extent can an
encounter with the work of Foucault open the possibility of self-
transformation, of thinking differently?

NOTES

1. For a very good collection of critical essays on the work of Foucault, see David
   Couzens Hoy (ed.), *Foucault: A Critical Reader* (Oxford: Basil Blackwell, 1986).
2. Many of the arguments against Foucault that follow are taken from J. G.
   Merquior, *Foucault* (London: Fontana Press/Collins, 1985).
3. Ibid, p. 159.
4. For a more specific criticism of Merquior's reading of Foucault, see Paul Bové's
   comments in the Introduction to G. Deleuze, *Foucault*, trans. Seán Hand
   (Minneapolis: University of Minnesota Press, 1990), pp. viii and xviii; and
   Barker, op. cit., *Michel Foucault: Subversions of the Subject*, p. 42.
5. It is a great pity that Merquior was not at the Department of Philosophy at the
   University of Sydney from 1975–85. There is still an important story to be told
   there.
6. But even here a further trap awaits: the phrase Anglo-American philosophy
   slips easily off the keyboard, imag[in]ing a clearly defined cohesive area of
   philosophical theory which we all intuitively know and share. However, as in
   the case of postmodernism, poststructuralism and feminism, so too for Anglo-
   American philosophy. Each of these words is nominal and represents a variety
   of positions that are often opposed if not completely antithetical to each other.
7. Entire disciplinary theoretical regimes can be broken apart and their fragments
   redistributed elsewhere, as in the example of phrenology at the beginning of the
   twentieth century.
8. See Chapter 3.
9. Descartes, op. cit., pp. 79–130. It is interesting that the actual title of this work
   is *The Discourse on the Method of Rightly Conducting Reason*, which serves to
   emphasis the significance and relevance of this point.
10. And not just contemporaries: it is also the object of much of the work of
    Nietzsche and Heidegger.

11. Derrida has suggested that what is attributed to Descartes' method, and what is not, is more ambiguous than this. See J. Derrida, *Writing and Difference*, trans. Alan Bass (Chicago: The University of Chicago Press, 1978), 'The Cogito and the History of Madness'. At this point, at a general level Foucault is probably standing a good deal closer to Merquior than the latter would like.

12. This is not just something that applies to philosophy as a discipline that should be seen as a particular effect of the university, which is a 'machine' for producing disciplinary regimes.

13. It could be argued that now in Australia, at least some of the universities that have adopted the business/professionalising university model are going against this trend. However, this involves developing closer connections with a changing educational bureaucracy, itself a disciplinary regime in need of analysis.

14. Foucault, *Foucault Live: Collected Interviews, 1961–1984*, ed. Sylvère Lotringer (New York: Semiotext(e), 1996), p. 69.

15. This is not to say that the position of students and academics is analogous; it is not. There are completely different sets of interests operating here.

16. Merquior is unable to think against the work of Foucault, because the paradigm within which he is working ensures that he thinks only about the work of Foucault without ever touching him, or even getting close – Merquior masters Foucault – in order to exclude this body from his own philosophical canon. Perhaps there is more than a little irony in the fact that Merquior's book on Foucault is part of the Fontana Modern Masters Series. For more on 'thinking against', see Heidegger, *Basic Writings*, ed. David Farrell Krell (London: Routledge, 1993), Letter on Humanism, pp. 213–65.

17. This is the basis of theory as diagnosis.

18. Is not examining these very things one of the major theoretical connections between Foucault, Nietzsche and Heidegger?

19. Deleuze, op. cit., *Foucault*. Deleuze's analysis of Foucault's work serves to provide the conditions for an encounter which fundamentally expands the work of Foucault in order that Deleuze may add further critical force to his own work – a force that involves Deleuze's own self-elaboration. This is an expansive encounter which resists a shorthand summary and commentary.

20. Based on P. Barker, 'Foucault's' Sublime: E-mail to Postumius Terentianus', in Claire O'Farrell (ed.), *Foucault: The Legacy* (Brisbane: Queensland University of Technology, 1997). For a collection of important essays on the sublime, see Jeffrey S. Librett (trans.), *Of the Sublime: Presence in Question* (New York: State University of New York Press, 1993).

21. Longinus, *Longinus on Elevation of Style*, trans. T. G. Tucker (Melbourne: Melbourne University Press, 1935), p. 5.

22. See Kant, *Observations on the Feeling of the Beautiful and the Sublime*, trans. John T. Goldthwait (Berkeley: University of California Press, 1991). Kant allows for there to be three kinds of sublime; the third – the splendid sublime – incorporates a certain beauty, however the fundamental opposition is still the beautiful and the sublime, as is suggested by the title of the work. Page 46:

> Finer feeling, which we now wish to consider, is chiefly of two kinds, the feeling of the *sublime* and that of the *beautiful*. The stirring of each is pleasant in different ways ... In order that the former impression could occur to us in due strength, we must have a *feeling of the sublime*, and, in order to enjoy the latter well, a *feeling of the beautiful*. Tall oaks and lonely shadows in a sacred grove are sublime; flower beds, low hedges and trees trimmed in

figures are beautiful. Night is sublime, day is beautiful. Temperaments that possess a feeling for the sublime are drawn gradually, by the quiet stillness of a summer evening as the shimmering light of the stars breaks through the brown shadows of night and the lonely moon rises into view, into high feelings of friendship, of disdain for the world, of eternity. The shining day stimulates busy fervor and a feeling of gaiety. The sublime *moves*, the beautiful *charms*. The mien of a man who is undergoing the full feeling of the sublime is earnest, sometimes rigid and astonished. On the other hand the lively sensation of the beautiful proclaims itself through shining cheerfulness in the eyes, through smiling features, and often through audible mirth. The sublime is in turn of different kinds. Its feeling is sometimes accompanied with a certain dread, or melancholy; in some cases merely with quiet wonder; and in still others with a beauty completely pervading a sublime plan. The first I shall call the *terrifying sublime*, the second the *noble*, and the third the *splendid*. Deep loneliness is sublime, but in a way that stirs terror.

See also E. Burke, *A Philosophical Enquiry into the Origin of our Ideas of the Sublime and Beautiful*, ed. J. T. Boulton (London: Routledge and Kegan Paul, 1958). See the Preface to the First Edition, p. 1: 'He [Burke] observed that the ideas of the sublime and beautiful were frequently confounded; and that both were indiscriminately applied to things greatly differing, and sometimes of natures directly opposite. Even Longinus, in his incomparable discourse upon a part of this subject, has comprehended things extremely repugnant to each other, under one common name of the *Sublime*.'

23. Longinus, op. cit., p. 12.
24. Ibid., p. 28.
25. Ibid., p. 52.
26. Ibid., p. 34.
27. Figures of 'thought' are: insistence, extenuation, hyperbole, irony, question-form, correction of oneself, aposiopesis. Those of expression are: repetition, antithesis, asyndeta, play on words and so on. But a real distinction between the two classes is scarcely possible.
28. Foucault, op. cit., *The Foucault Reader*, 'What is Enlightenment?', p. 45. It is of note that later discussions of the sublime (including this one) ignore the conceptualising of 'sound' in the sublime and only seem to focus on the visual. See Librett, op. cit., Michel Deguy, 'The Discourse of Exaltation', pp. 10–11. See also G. Deleuze and F. Guattari, *A Thousand Plateaus*, trans. B. Massumi (Minneapolis: University of Minnesota Press, 1987), 'Of the Refrain', p. 310.
29. M. Foucault and M. Blanchot, *Foucault/Blanchot* (New York: Zone Books, 1987), p. 27. I am not suggesting that they are all exactly the same concept but that they are framed by similar questions.
30. This is the moment of Heidegger's entry. See Heidegger, *Basic Writings*, op. cit., 'The Origin of the Work of Art', p. 178.
31. Hence the importance of Zarathustra's descent from the mountain. Above everything else, Zarathustra is a geographer!
32. Dreyfus and Rabinow, op. cit., *Michel Foucault: Beyond Structuralism and Hermeneutics*, p. 208.
33. This is the basis of a nominalist critique of both metaphysics and realism.
34. Once again, these relations are not dialectical but are amplifications and magnifications.
35. The dangerous nature of the sublime is typified by the work of Sade. See

Marquis de Sade, *Philosophy in the Bedroom and Other Writings* (New York: Grove Press, 1965), pp. 741–2:

> Terrified, Madame de Lorsange begs her sister to make all haste and close the shutters; anxious to calm her, Thérèse dashes to the windows which are already being broken; she would do battle with the wind, she gives a minute's fight, is driven back and at that instant a blazing thunder bolt reaches her where she stands in the middle of the room . . . transfixes her.
>
> Madame de Lorsange emits a terrible cry and falls in a faint; Monsieur de Corville calls for help, attentions are given each woman, Madame de Lorsange is revived, but the unhappy Thérèse has been struck in such wise hope itself can no longer subsist for her; the lightning entered her right breast, found the heart, and after having consumed her chest and face, burst out through her belly. The miserable thing was hideous to look upon; Monsieur de Corville orders that she be borne away.
>
> . . . The prosperity of Crime is but an ordeal to which Providence would expose Virtue, it is like unto the lightning, whose traitorous brilliancies but for an instant embellish the atmosphere, in order to hurl into death's very deeps the luckless one they have dazzled.

36. Foucault, op. cit., *Language, Counter-Memory, Practice*, 'Preface to Transgression', pp. 34–5.
37. Dreyfus and Rabinow op. cit., *Michel Foucault: Beyond Structuralism and Hermeneutics*, 'The Subject and Power', p. 212. See also Chapter 3 of this book, 'To Discipline and Subject'.
38. Foucault, op. cit., *The Foucault Reader*, 'What is Enlightenment?', p. 45. (For more on this, see Chapter 4.)
39. Ibid., p. 46.
40. This is an index of the modern.
41. Foucault, op. cit., *Death and the Labyrinth*, 'Postscript: An Interview with Michel Foucault', p. 182.
42. Nietzsche, *Daybreak – Thoughts on the Prejudices of Morality*, trans. R. J. Hollingdale (Cambridge: Cambridge University Press, 1983), p. 221.

7

BETWEEN DEATH – OBLITERATION

Another sunny day in Brisbane. Encountering one blue-sky day after another can become a matter of terrible endurance. Orleigh Park is magnificent. Dogs runramble along trying to appropriate food from grass-sat children with whom they have no familial connections, while their owners look down at the lead in their hand – and wish it was connected to its proper dog-object. Across the river at the Guyatt Park pontoon scholars embark and disembark, 'toing and froing' from the university. It is autumn now, the early mornings are cooler and the evenings are starting to draw in. In the fading light, things become less shadowy but more profusely obscure.

Soon there will be an anniversary. Two years of being in Brisbane – it will be quickly followed by another two years – writing this book. During that time, many things have changed and many transformations have been made – and all of them are to be found in these few pages concerning the work of Michel Foucault. It has been a time of many meetings, companionship and friendship, along the way – the way to this last chapter, the last word, the last full stop of this work.

I name some of those who have passed-speaking touching through me: 'Alice' in the park, Francisco Ascui, Martin Ball, Ben, Yvette Blackwood, Ann Brooks, Rebecca Butterworth, Carrie, Chris, Connie, Craig, Classical Dan, Pam Dennison, Diana, Julie Douglas, Nena-Fay, Fluted-Kathy, Jackie, Jan, John Frow, Zoe Furmin, Gerard, Henk, Henry Hicks, Johnny, John Hill, Larry, Lucy, Martin, Rob Miazek, Mira, Claire O'Farrell, Dan O'Neil, Pandora, Robin Ratcliffe, 'Paulo' Reilley, Stu Robinson, Angela Rockel, Richard Sampson, Scott, Eva-Marie Seeto, David Simpson, Peter Thomas, Tony Thwaites, Graeme Turner, David Whatson, Yani. And, all those broken conversation-people at Cafe Bohemia, on the ferry to St Lucia, on the bus, in the street on Hardgrave Road – at the Boundary Hotel on Saturday afternoons 'without boundaries'. Fragments of them intersect this work – they have a certain relation to its form, where it draws out – and where it folds in. As well as this, they exist within their own multiple forming lines: students, painters, sculptors, lovers, friends, professors, prostitutes, junkies, mothers, fathers, dealers, musicians, poets, teachers . . . brothers/sisters-daughters/sons . . .

Which was more important? Dinner with John Frow, where we spoke of Foucault, Deleuze and the will to knowledge and when John graciously drew out issues that remain in this work unacknowledged? Presenting a paper to the English Department at the University of Queensland, listening to Bec wrestle with time, or hearing Alice laugh Foucault, with the infectious, confident nervousness of one deeply lost in the world . . .? Reading *The History of Sexuality, Volume 1* one more time or overhearing a disembodied voice at Cafe Bohemia say: 'men don't know how to fuck women – only mothers or daughters. A daughter who will be their mother – a mother who will be their daughter. It's all the same. I tell them I won't be anyone's mother or daughter . . .'?

When you write a book, things change . . . this does not necessarily have to be framed as a Platonic problem . . . the location of stable foundations may not be important . . . To write is to write from within a problematic of change. To write is to encounter limits – the limit of the keyboard, the limit of the ink sprayed across the page or the heat that burns images into it. To write is to encounter resistances, to write is to scratch – to mark – to draw things out. It is to think against, to be drawn into – it is to encounter bodies, borders, boundaries, limits – it is to breathe heavily and deeply – it is to feel the sound of your own pulse, hear your heartbeat – it is to give witness to your own transformations and those of others. It is to reformulate, to redraft and finally to come to a full stop in order to meet publishing deadlines and the limit-reality of book production.

It is to face up to the impossible border of the cover, to place these marks, these scratchings within these borders so they can be circulated and distributed and undertake their unrestrained serial modification. It is to understand that divisions between inside and outside make no sense in books or in life and death – life on the inside and death on the outside. The one folding in, the other drawing out. Death obliteration. Life obliteration. It is a question of the linearity of language. Of death occurring faster – on a different line or register – than language.

Like Alice's be-coming smile. Languid. Implacable. Sensoriously beautiful. Censoriously beautiful. A mask. A frozen moment – the necrophiliac object[ive]. Alice's smile is the unrepresentable of language – the smile of the already dead – her pupils roll upwards and she reveals the translucent whites of her eyes. She stammers fragments of language that mean nothing but signify everything, as she draws into herself and then explodes and disperses across every surface of her material existences. The outside folds in as the inside folds out – one draws the line of the other – merges with, into, onto the others.

Alice's smile cuts across two axes – inside/outside – death/life. These axes are anchoring points, coherences that touch against us when we write-die, face our own death – obliteration. They exist in a complex interrelation – against which self and other are articulated – as the possibility of any experience, and they provide the folding curve which links theorising and being in the world. It is against the already there (inside – outside: the event of death) that we find and lose ourselves, and elaborate the transformations which we draw out of/for our identities.

I remember the precise moment when a long-lasting anxiety attack began.[1] It was 18 October 1994, and a list of speakers for a conference at which I had promised to present a paper had just been received. The series of names drew out the borders of the 'speaking' space and framed two questions for me: how would it be possible to be at home amid such company, and why did it engender such anxiety? Then slowly it became clear that this anxiety somehow related to the issue of 'performance' and perhaps demanded a return to the Philosophy of Language or Psychoanalysis. A return to the Performative or the Performance.

But where does the performance take place – as the throat dries, the heart pumps wildly, the capillaries flush red just under the surface of the skin and small droplets of sweat trickle down the neck? A performance and an anxiety that is multi-dimensional – surfaces, folds and a series of subtle surface interrelations as anxiety is drawn out 'on' the body – a diagram of interiority, yet completely visible on the surface.

How can this interior/exterior relation be theorised? Is it indeed a journey, a passage, a passageway from interior to exterior and back to interior where the surface of the body is a border that cannot be crossed but must force a return, that cannot be stepped beyond? Does the surface of the body act as a reflective wall that turns the body back into itself, or does the surface of the body act to diagram a series of multiple relations? Perhaps this is something that can be rethought by examining three examples that draw out aspects of this issue, and which are illustrations that figure out the question of interiority and exteriority, depth and surface, and which envisage a journey and a return.

The first example is from the *Discourse on Method*.² The *Discourse on Method* is in large part an apologia for a work called *The World* which Descartes apparently destroyed before publication. In the *Discourse on Method*, Descartes frequently refers to this absent text where all matters of things were proved but were never brought to the light of day – to the surface.³ In Section V of the *Discourse on Method*, Descartes summarises the content of this absent work in the terms of an imaginary theoretical space, and details the circulatory system belonging to imaginary bodies.⁴

He begins his lesson in anatomy with an examination of the heart and arteries, by exploring the two cavities of the heart, one being the *vena cava*.⁵ From the *vena cava* he follows the arterial vein through to the lungs, and then the windpipe and the valves of the heart, and then he develops his account of the mechanical operation of the heart. He traces the blood to the extremities of the arteries and notes how valves are arranged in the veins to stop the blood flowing backwards. He then examines how, when an artery is cut, the blood 'issues' forth on the surface of the body, and discusses the nerves, muscles and animal spirits and changes in the brain, finally suggesting

> [how] light, sounds, smells, tastes, heat and all other qualities pertaining to external objects are able to imprint on it various ideas by the intervention of the senses; how hunger, thirst and other internal affections can also convey their impressions upon it; what should be regarded as the 'common sense' by which these ideas are received, and what is meant by the memory which retains them . . .⁶

Here an uncertain tone makes its way into Descartes' analysis. He has arrived at the surfaces of the body, those outside/inside folds where the body encounters exteriority: sight, sound, smell and so on, and at once imposes an anxious qualification on their operation by introducing the famous *automaton* argument, raising the question of how we can we tell the difference between an *automaton* (a clockwork machine resembling a man) and a 'real man'.

Descartes argues that there are two ways of doing this. First, only 'men' have a capacity for speech because a machine cannot arrange its speech 'in various ways, in order to reply appropriately to every-thing that may be said in its presence, as even the lowest type of man can do'. Second, machines 'did not act from knowledge, but only from the disposition of their organs'. In utilising a combination of linguistic performance, and acting on the basis of self-knowledge derived from the *Cogito*, Descartes presupposes a return to the performance of language to a standard that implies rational thought, in the face of extreme sceptical anxiety – how can I know the (R)eal?

In the *Discourse on Method*, Descartes undertakes a journey from interiority to exteriority and back to interiority. The uncertainty of the experience of the surface and its relations with exteriority drive him back to the principles of abstract interiority, while at the same time the moment of this return is constructed with reference to anxiety and performance, which then remain lying in wait to draw in those who might follow.

Plato's allegory of the cave in the *Republic* can also be read as a journey from interiority to exteriority and back again. The Platonic prisoners are chained up with their backs to the fire so they can only see shadowy representations of what passes upon a pathway behind them. One of them is released and is forced to turn around to be dazzled by the fire, and slowly and inexorably undertakes the journey to the opening of the cave onto the (R)eal world. Passing by the dazzling light of the fire, he eventually reaches the surface and encounters the Sun and Enlightenment, and filled with inspiration returns down the passageway to the cave, only to meet the ridicule and scorn of the other prisoners.

> They would laugh at him and say that he had gone up only to come back with his sight ruined: it was worth no one's while even to attempt the ascent. If they could lay hands on the man who was trying to set them free and lead them up, they would kill him.[7]

Many questions remain unanswered. How does the first prisoner come to be released? Who forces him to turn around? How does the first step occur? What happens to the one who releases him? Why does he return to interiority? – not, as in the case of Descartes, because of a scepticism about the interaction of the surfaces of the body with other objects or people, but because he felt sorry for them in their ignorance of their relation to their state of interiority. He understands that the prisoners think the shadows on the wall are all there, is but he knows more than this. The one who can return always knows the truth, and because of this truth he can no longer play the shadow game, and receives the odium of the other prisoners which is the cause of his anxiety. In the face of this, he returns to play games of truth instead of shadow games and to perform philosophy in a state of acute anxiety, fearing attack from the other prisoners. Philosophy, Performance and Anxiety return.

In the book *Volatile Bodies*, we also find a journey, a journey from interiority to exteriority and back.[8] The book is in four divisions: Introduction, The Inside Out, The Outside In, and Sexual Difference. Therefore the articulation of Sexual Difference is 'prefigured' by the journey from the Inside Out to the Outside In. This general structure is accompanied by the key metaphor of the Möbius strip.

The Möbius strip can be described as a strip of paper with a twist in it with the ends joined together. This allows both sides of the strip to be traced continuously. However, this tracing can also be read as a journey or movement, that passes from inside to outside and outside to inside, each point of return having to negotiate the twist. We also learn from the Introduction that the book is framed around a wager, a wager being 'something laid down and hazarded on the issue of an uncertain event; a stake'. If we continue down the reductive path of definition, we learn that a stake is that which is placed at hazard. Or, as a verb, to stake – to impale (a person) on a stake.

In the context of the Introduction to *Volatile Bodies*, it can be argued that 'stake' serves a double purpose. On the one hand, it recounts a certain relation of performance and anxiety that emerges from the relation between the writer of *Volatile Bodies* and the text, while on the other *Volatile Bodies* also involves a relation to performance and anxiety, that emerges from a staking of the ground and a folding inwards of the surface which drives it towards interiority.

These three examples can be drawn together. Each of them describes the relation between interiority and exteriority in terms of a double movement. The First Movement is from inside to outside, the Second Movement is from outside to inside and between the first and the second movement is the step of the Return. The step (*pas*) around and back that turns on a double moment of negation – not inside – not outside. Not A, not B. A step that prior to the moment of the return momentarily hovers over an abyss at the border, at the frontier, where to keep on going beyond the surface would be to disperse oneself.

The linked problematic of step and return is important if we wish to analyse the relation between interior and exterior in terms of an inside/outside oscillation, and is not helped by the metaphor of the Möbius strip where the elision of the return under the twist – which brings you back to the same point – only serves to mask the significance of the problematic of step and return. Precisely what needs to be put into question is the critical correlation between step (*pas*), return, and the way the twist functions to mask the moment of step/return. To briefly summarise and raise some further issues:

1. The return becomes a critical moment in the examination of the inside and the outside and raises the possibility of an analysis that might also include the politics of the return.
2. The question 'why it is that interiority retains its primacy?' could be raised alongside another, 'why is interiority the place of the first step (*pas*)?'
3. Any analysis of interiority and the journey to the surface needs to take account of the meaning of to surface, or surfacing. Namely, that which surfaces has previously gone down or under. This raises a further problem: is there a possibility of restoring the primacy of the surface of exteriority that does not depend on simply reversing the binary of interiority/exteriority?[9]
4. In what way could the relation of the body to Performance and Anxiety be elaborated?[10]
5. We should analyse the relation of the body to difference and repetition. The body is that cluster or assemblage that repeats itself, and yet is different from moment to moment.[11] This analysis involves a theory of distance and proximity or magnitude/amplification.
6. We need to encounter the failure of the return to interiority – that going beyond the border, of making one more step and encountering Other bodies/surfaces and dispersal, death/obliteration.[12]
7. We need to understand that the multiplicity of the body exists at various times/speeds. For example, the time of the virus is altogether quite different from the time of bone growth.[13]

Where does all this take us? Do we have any other alternative than to go down a predictable path in the history of philosophy, and attempt to develop a vocabulary that will allow us to draw the body differently? This transient body that, irrespective of the adoption of techniques of shaping or altering, changes anyway. Its surfaces extend, distend – its appearance regularly alters in so many ways. It gets cut, marked, scarred. It heals, and in its healing it reshapes itself. It overlaps and interconnects with others, folds back on itself. It goes grey, patchy, flaky, oily. On the whole, the body is not a 'whole' but a complex of interrelated events.

In the face of this, if we are not either to refer it back to an ide- alised unitary form with all its Platonic overtones, or allow it to be intersected by the problematic of dualism, perhaps it can be rethought on the model of *n*-dimensional surface relations. This would be to recognise that the skin is not just on the surface, or even in the surface. *It* is a surface and like all other surfaces relates vertically and horizontally in all directions.[14]

This suggests that the principle of inversion which emerges from my reading of *Volatile Bodies* is an important first step that draws out the beginning of a further series of investigations. 'Inversion – *turning upside down; the folding back of stratified rocks on each other; a reversal of position order and sequence or relation; invert – to turn in, to turn outside in, hence to turn the opposite way.*' We cannot afford to be locked into the narrowing reductive limitation of the inverse. A literary binary folding of the outside and the inside together as the inverse draws a mask over the return, the step around and back.

How would it be possible to sketch a diagram that would draw us down from surface to interior? On what basis could such a diagram find its points of attachment, its points of coherence? Perhaps in no more than attempting to theorise the possibility of the first move- ment, the first step – crossing the first incremental space which is only possible by analysing the schema: identity, difference and return.

There is a certain style in which such difficult work can be undertaken. It can take the form of an apologia, for its inadequacies claiming 'but it is only work in progress'. However, putting up a mask of disingenuous apologetic humility in this way can serve to cover over a problematic relation to the whole question of work in progress. It gestures towards a progressive difference from, and return to, something that is not quite absolutely and certainly it, which implies that work, if it is to be *Work*, *really* has a telos and is hurtling toward that millennial ending when it will be clear, complete, closed, full.

Therefore, it can be argued that there is a relation between work and progress, completed work, and a certain style which, in a gesture towards its completion, points to a characteristic unity with itself, and yet a certain reticence can be felt at accepting an opposition between work in progress and incomplete work, and then simply attempting to reverse it.

Does the experience of this reticence offer an opportunity to think of one's work as being neither in progress, nor complete, nor unfinished – but simply as work 'at hand'? The 'at hand' refuses the incrementalism of accumulating progress, and allows a pointed focus on the issue of identity, difference and coming back, without having to face up to the issue of the possibility of work having a unity with itself and its onto-theological consequences.

These question are acutely manifest in the *Phenomenology of Spirit*, where we are presented with a tracing of how a work can be complete and unified unto itself.[15] The consequence of this is felt at the moment of the arrival of Absolute Spirit, when the work has incorporated into itself every possibility or potentiality that it ever had, which is why it is 'completed' work. It is totally encompassing, leaving nothing outside its economy, with the emphasis being placed on the 'absolute' rather than the 'spirit'. This is nothing less than a question of theology, albeit disguised under the apparently arbitrary operation of progressive history and the Work in Progress.

This can be represented by the formula A=A, which is one of the fundamental formulations of Western Logic. However, this formula also operates at the level of a 'concealing' because

> The formula A=A speaks of equality. It doesn't define A as the same. The common formulation of the principle of identity thus conceals precisely what the principle is trying to say: A is A, that is, every A is itself the same.[16]

In the formula A=A, there is a moment of collapse whereby A falls back in on itself. However, this concealing and its collapse also point to something else. When we say that A is A, or that every A is itself the same, we are suggesting that every A is the same with itself.[17] The 'with' and the 'the' fuse together to provide the moment of concealing. What can be drawn out of this is that the principle of identity, in terms of completion, appears to gesture towards an all-inclusive fullness, but in fact conceals a moment of reductivity, as this identity is reduced to a repetition of the same with itself. We might say that this is *the* phallic moment par excellence.[18]

In this moment, identity becomes the reduction of the possibility of difference, a reduction that is concealed by the history of Western metaphysics and its theology of the same.[19] There is another implication of this process to be thought, which is its resistance to temporality. While the formula A=A implies a linear progression that must necessarily be within the temporal reinterpretation of this, as A is in fact A, the same with itself, it resists any movement, which is the first condition of temporality. So, because it is complete unto itself, it is resistant to time and history. This is one of the very beautiful ironies of Absolute Spirit: nothing much can happen when it arrives.

One can say, in terms of the identity of the same, that the more temporality goes forward according to the traditional history of metaphysics, the more it reduces to the same.[20] The further you go on in time, the more you know about yourself in the sense of accumulation and the more you are reduced to an identity of the one. This then reinforces that we are dealing with a fundamentally theological question. Therefore, it might be pleasurable to ask how it is possible to turn this theological moment around, and reveal identity and difference as something other. Perhaps this task can then be broken down into:

1. forcing a transition from 'with' to 'between' – which parallels a movement from the identity of the same to irreducible difference;
2. dealing with the question of the step back and the turn around;
3. reformulating the background of an analysis of a discontinuous notion of temporality.

With this task in mind, the issues of identity, difference and the return can be opened up by examining the text *Rebecca* by Daphne du Maurier.

> Last night I dreamt I went to Manderley again. It seemed to me I stood by the iron gate leading to the drive, and for a while I could not enter, for the way was barred to me. There was a padlock and a chain upon the gate. I called in my dream to the lodge-keeper, and had no answer, and peering closer through the rusted spokes of the gate I saw that the lodge was uninhabited.[21]

The narrator goes on to explain that she and her partner are in exile from England, living in a small 'foreign' hotel, and alludes to a tragic and destructive event that had happened to the stately old home of Manderley. For the first-time reader, an opening is made into the future possibility of the book – through the memory of the narrator as the narration folds back from the past into the future and back to the past – in a similar way to that reductive Hegelian moment that was mentioned earlier in relation to the identity of the same.

The narrator and the reader's consciousness will be linked, reduced to the same through the vehicle of the narrative strategy. Yet there is a curious looping effect in the construction of *Rebecca*, because the introduction to the novel takes on an entirely new set of meanings after it has been read. At the end of *Rebecca*, what cries out with great insistence is that the introductory pages be reread, and in this rereading they are found to be irreducibly different. In this way, the structure of *Rebecca* offers the possibility of resistance to that theological moment that I alluded to earlier, and the structure of this resistance finds its organising principle in the return – the coming back.

Indeed, *Rebecca* is a novel about coming back, about returning. We may never be able to go back – but we can always come back. The structuring metaphor for coming back is the name of Rebecca's little yacht *Je Reviens*, which the narrator tells us means 'I come back'. She continues: 'Yes, I suppose it was quite a good name for a boat. Only it had not been for that particular boat which would never come back again.'[22]

The name of this little yacht and its *coming back* opens up the possibility of resistance to a certain style of criticism that views 'the text' as being always in some sense or other the same. This view holds that a text can always ultimately be reduced to a single set of meanings be they formal, intentional, biographical or otherwise, which presupposes that it can be forced into a singular identity with itself – the identity of the same.

An alternative view might suggest that a text is polysemic and that meaning can be endlessly constructed. In itself, this does not necessarily resist reduction to the same, because one might still presuppose the possibility of infinite accumulation of interpretations. Such a process would take us back to the Hegelian model of the unfolding of the absolute through a progressive accumulative history, in this case of literary criticism.[23]

However, one of the difficulties with both the positions which I have outlined is that neither has anything to say about coming back to the text, about the return. Indeed, returning to a text, as one so often does, does not seem to have been problematised very much at all.[24] This takes us back to the name of Rebecca's yacht, *Je Reviens*, and the ironic stance of the narrator who, speaking through a fold in time, already knows that the yacht does come back – and therefore is quite appropriately named – even as she tells us that this boat will never come back.

If the event of reading the opening chapter of *Rebecca* once, and then again after we have completed the novel, is rethought, this commits us to drawing out the moment of coming back. Would this coming back belong to the category of A=A, as if the two events are connected by a 'with', the reductive principle of identity, or can it be more properly thought as being modulated by the principle of irreducible difference, where what is drawn out is the 'betweenness' of the two events? Could it be that in this return, this coming back, *the between* intervenes between the two events and ensures that each is irreducible in terms of the other? This would be an irreducibility that presupposes a space of absolute difference, neither as lack nor as fullness but as unmediated differentiation, which would create an irreducible space between two events, and offer the possibility of establishing a critique of the theological underpinning of Western metaphysics and its identity of the same.[25]

One way of accomplishing this and recognising this irreducible space might be to undertake the step back and turn around – to step back from the between of two events and turn around and face oneself. In this facing, what is evident is the connection between the irreducibility of events and the irreducibility of one's own relation to oneself, from moment to moment. In this way, irreducible recognition becomes the moment of turning around, of facing oneself. However, could it not be argued that to step back and turn around and face oneself reinforces the visual undercurrent of Western metaphysics and its grounding *Cogito*? Perhaps this takes a little more thought.[26]

Let us recollect the touch of our fingertips on the skin of a lover, that moment of the tracing of identities, when each folds into the folds of the other. That rush of time sometimes compressed, sometimes drawn out. Yet even amid the eroticised intensification of pleasure, does not the thought of *the between* insist?[27] That is, in life the irreducible is ever-present and the irreducible is *the between* by another name. A *between* that presupposes the possibility of a step back to touch oneself, which is the moment of coming back and at the same time is the assertion of irreducibility. Perhaps it is *being between* that provides the murmurings of a possible critique of Western metaphysics? In the absence of the face as unitary sight/site of accumulation and identity, what remains is just another series of surfaces touching themselves as they touch the other. Neither here nor there, simultaneously both present and absent – *between*.[28]

Let us come back to the image of Rebecca's little yacht *Je Reviens*, lying under the sea near Manderley complete with the bleached bones of Rebecca, caught between death and death, preparing to be more insistent than ever. Meanwhile, in Manderley the new Mrs De Winter is caught between her former name, which we are never told, her position as the second Mrs De Winter, and her being overwhelmed by the 'presence' of the dead Rebecca (the first Mrs De Winter). Indeed, all the characters in *Rebecca* participate in so many betweens that *the between* overwhelms the possibility of 'with' or 'and'.

The between becomes the organising structure of the narrative, even at that moment when the second Mrs De Winter/narrator appears at the fancy-dress ball in exactly the same gown as Rebecca had worn the year before. It is *the between* that structures the recognition that she is not Rebecca, and yet creates a relation where she and Rebecca fold into each other to produce anxiety and anger in the usually pleasant (if taciturn) Maxim De Winter. The movement and oscillation in *the between* allows for an alternative ontology to that of the 'same', its incorporation of the principle of reductive identity of A=A and its theological reassertion of 'with'.

As for Rebecca, she who comes back from under the sea, from between death and death, her presence is always and already still acting on the characters at Manderley. Her coming back places her between them all again with greater intensity, but as we are to learn she was already between death and death even before she went to the bottom of the sea. From the moment she learned that she had inoperable cancer, Rebecca chose to conjure up a death that would forever place her between Maxim De Winter and herself. She engineered to have him kill her.

Between them all Rebecca lay, and still lies even after we have read the novel once and accept its insistent injunction to come back to the beginning one more time. We are driven to position ourselves between the first and second reading and then perhaps a third and fourth, and indeed this is a function of being a being between language. As Foucault suggests, we exist *between* the already saids, between the possibility of what can be said, of what has been said. This saying contains within it the embodiment of language, in the blood, in the cells, in the fingertips, in the matrix that constitutes what it is to be a human being today.

Well, perhaps this is all a bit much bringing *Identity and Difference* and *Rebecca* together in this way. To structure such a forced link between the proper names of Heidegger and Du Maurier and imagine that *Rebecca* is an extended thought on the principle of identity and difference, and coming back – and then to draw out from it the first unsteady step towards an elaboration of the principle of *the between*.

However, further support for Du Maurier's interest in *coming back* and *the between* can be found in *My Cousin Rachel*, which begins and ends with the same two sentences: 'They used to hang men at Four Turnings in the old days. Not any more, though.'[29] Perhaps more obviously than *Rebecca*, this novel lies between this coming back and the set of meanings attached to these two sentences, which at the end of the novel are quite different from those attached to them at its beginning. Rather than going on to analyse the fusing of the narrator's identity with that of his dead uncle, and the unexpected arrival of letters which insist on coming back even from the dead, it might be more useful at this point to take up the third of the issues which it was suggested frame any analysis of identity, difference and return: reformulating the background of an analysis of a discontinuous notion of temporality.

A continuous notion of temporality would be dependent upon a conceptualising of temporality that is associated with a continuous progression of temporal events along a single plane, and which unfolds alongside a progressing consciousness – a *Cogito*. The horizon may shift, but we know where we are going in an ever-continuing process of the accumulation of knowledge and 'self'-awareness. This experience of temporality is one founded on the history of Western metaphysics and the experience of the temporal as a continuous unfolding. But perhaps it is time once again to think more about temporality. In particular, we need to reassociate it with its cognate – temporary. For here, there is a gesture that points to the temporal as temporary – as disrupted – as dissociated and discontinuous. Indeed, it is in the temporary quality of the temporal that we find the experience of irreducibility and *the between*.

All moments must be irreducible to each other, or the event of specific or particular recognition would be impossible.[30] *The between* separates temporal moments and locks them into a series of events that are irreducible to each other. This parallels a fragmented structure of consciousness as one of irreducible identity in difference, and provides an alternative account of what it is to be, to that of the synthesised, unified, progressing consciousness. This draws out an opening of the possibility of a non-reductive interaction between self and other, between self and text – where self is but a momentary touching against, and not the site/sight of accumulated unfolding knowledge, referring to a single locus and identity.

Let us come back to some of the points that have already been drawn out. It was argued that the concept of work in progress implied a moment of completion, of unity and stasis. Hegel's *The*

Phenomenology of Spirit was offered as an example of a work that at the moment of the unfolding of Absolute Spirit becomes complete and unified unto itself. These two thoughts were drawn together by taking from Heidegger his critique of the formula A=A, and adopting his suggestion that this conceals the principle of 'with' whereby each A collapses into each other('s) identical A.

It is in this reductive collapse that a *Cogito* grounds itself, and in this grounding is able to reduce the other to that which it recognises as being identical with itself. This is the subject that colonises, and it should not be forgotten that Descartes' methodology is elaborated in the 'autobiographical' genre (which I have discussed elsewhere) and that Descartes was and perhaps always remained a soldier- adventurer, a specialist at inducing the capture/death of the other (and in death perhaps there is not much difference?).[31]

It was argued that the logical structure A=A resists specific moments of time and particular histories because every movement forwards is always also a movement to the Absolute, a 'timeless' space because it exists in the complete unity of itself with itself. The possibility of a critique of the self-identifying *Cogito* and the reductive a-temporal logic of 'A is the same with A' was raised by thinking through three principles in *Identity and Difference* and *Rebecca* which would:

1. force a transition from 'with' to 'between';
2. deal with the question of the step back and the turn around;
3. reformulate the background of an analysis of a discontinuous notion of temporality.

This has led to the difficult problem of coming back and its close association with irreducibility and *the between*. It has been implied that what is necessary is a shift in terminology from identity, difference and the return to *the between* and the irreducible.

Surely today in the modern world we live in *the between*. As we turn towards the world, we live between birth and death (in Heidegger's terminology) or, as I would prefer to say, between death and death. We live in a world of zombies, phantasms, ghosts and the hyper-real, a world of machine-men, cyberspace and human/animal viruses. Neither here nor there – neither present or absent – we are between things. Perhaps there is no set of relations that escapes *the between*. Between your touch and my skin, between surfaces, between bodies, between pleasures ... We can no longer say *I think therefore I am* without a smile – murmuring instead *between I am therefore I think?*[32]

The between allows for an irreducible difference between identities that resists colonial subjectification and subjection. *The between* clears the ground for the coming back, as *the between* is temporal, yet involves a temporality which oscillates all at once between past, present and future. Perhaps above all, *the between* fragments into be-and-tween. Small-b being. *The between* cannot be reduced to itself because it only exists as a relation. It is not substantial and can take on no reductive essentialism. The shift from *I think* to *between* offers a springing out of modernity and gestures towards the possibility of embracing irreducibility and drawing ourselves out of the mire of *identity and difference* and the return, towards *being between the irreducible presence of always coming back.*

Perhaps today we have before us an opening whereby we can resist the most oppressive injunction of Western metaphysics, A=A, and the politics of making a difference, by embracing being *between* and being difference, which allows for the possibility of a *non-differential* passing between the obliteration of death and death. Between ourselves and others there would then be only those delightful moments of the pleasure of being in the fold between self and other, of being between all things, stretched thin – a translucent membrane of *the between*.[33]

But at what moment would there be no return from surface to interior? At what moment would the exterior fold into the interior, or the interior into the exterior, and complete the oscillation of *the between*? Would this only be constituted by the possibility of the aporia of death? Of moving beyond being between surfaces into absolute exteriority/interiority/presence/absence?

Imagine how a jeweller makes wire. You take a larger-diameter wire than the one you want and force it through a template of the dimensions that you require by dragging it through a drawplate. Perhaps we can see ourselves drawn between surfaces by the aporia of the event of death, and so constituting a relation with interiority that initiates surface/death outside/inside oscillations? Perhaps it is from the possibility of the experience of the absolute outside/inside that we constitute the absolute other which we formulate through the outside/inside relation? Is our cultural drawplate the aporia of death, of becoming dispersed, of dissolution: obliteration – and is it this that draws us from the outside back to the inside at the moment of the return and marks the folding of the body on itself and others – being between outside and inside: surface and interiority?

In response to this, we can see the stabilising of the body as a political, cultural and economic event which lies on the surfaces of the body, induces stability and interiority, and which draws out the possibility of one more step, one more not I – where I was but am no more.[34] This leaves us in a position of being between moments of folding interaction, drawing surfaces – drawing bodies: drawing ourselves.

It has been raining continuously for two days. I spend the afternoon with a friend. We don't talk much. The silence is comforting. Sometimes she writes things down – sometimes she slips away into another world – I try not to intrude and call her back. At five o'clock we go for a walk. Sometimes we walk on opposite sides of the road. Sometimes we walk side by side, she points out features of gardens we pass – the rain streams down her face. We buy hot chips and walk down to Orleigh Park. The rain draws a hazy glow around the street lamps. She circuits a tree – I walk on. We lose each other for a while. I look up, she is beside me. She speaks – some of her words are lost against the rain. We walk in the road – there are no cars – it's too wet for cars. We are backstreetwalkers/crawlers.

I take off my hat so I can feel the rain in my hair – it streams down my face, misting my glasses. Unexpectedly we find ourselves on Hoogley Street – closer to where we were than we thought we should have been. We walk to 'Caravanserai' and have sambuca coffees. The glasses clink together – 'Companionship'. We sit there in silence, in the cafe-light each just smiling towards the other as we drip wet on the floor – her figure draws together, morphs and merges with Alice . . . often when things seem most real they are at their most fragmented and slippery fluid wet . . . we walk up Hardgrave Road, she mists out of sight through the rain towards town, in search of movies at the State Library . . .

I go home. I write this provisional closure for Chapter 7 – I hope that this one more coming back is not edited out . . . It has been a time of many births and deaths, all of them in this book. Many outside/inside folds, many being betweens: so many that I hesitate to place the last full stop, knowing perfectly well that every full stop presupposes the capital letter of the next word. A capital letter, an investing letter, a judicial letter, a dead letter – finding its meanings in my own death – finding its proper/propre place drawn out in multiple registrations between death-obliteration in voices that are neither Foucault's nor my own but which belong to all of us:

> Must I suppose that, in my discourse, it is not my own survival which is at stake? And that, by speaking, I do not exorcise my

death, but establish it; or rather, that I suppress all interiority, and yield my utterance to an outside which is so indifferent to my life, so *neutral,* that it knows no difference between my life and my death?[35]

NOTES

1. What follows in this chapter is based on an unpublished paper titled 'in vena cava: drawing bodies–drawing ourselves' that was presented at the *Culture/Sex/Economies* Conference at the University of Melbourne in December 1994. Two key terms are: *vena cava* and *draw*. Without reducing them to something less than they might be, I offer a rough definition intended rather to expand and multiply their possible meanings and the points they connect with. *Vena cava* – the name applied to either of the two large vessels that open into the right atrium of the heart. The word 'draw' has a multi-page entry in the Oxford English Dictionary; here are just a few of the meanings and derivatives: *Draw* – to pull, drag, tear, contract, shrink, weave, remove, displace, come, go, endure, suffer, take in, breathe, inhale, to attract by a force, to persuade, convert, to exercise allurement, to attract, to collect or assemble, to bring evil upon, to extract, to remove, to decide by chance, to separate, to leave undecided, to take water, to cause liquid to flow from a wound, to extract by suction, to cause a flow of blood, to promote suppuration of a poultice or blister.
2. Descartes, op. cit., *The Philosophical Works of Descartes, Volume 1.*
3. Although it exists as an absent phantasm in his corpus. See translators' note, Descartes, op. cit, Volume 1, p. 80.
4. Ibid., 'I resolved to leave all this world to their disputes, and to speak only of what would happen in a new world if God now created, somewhere in an imaginary space, matter sufficient wherewith to form it, and if He agitated in diverse ways, and without any order, the diverse portions of this matter, so that there resulted a chaos as confused as the poets ever feigned, and concluded His work by merely lending His concurrence to Nature in the usual way, leaving her act in accordance with the laws which He had established', p. 107. Early on in the *Discourse on the Method,* Descartes refers to it being treated as a history or fable.
5. Ibid., pp. 106–18.
6. Ibid., p. 115.
7. Plato, *The Republic of Plato*, trans. F. M. Cornford (Oxford: Clarendon Press, 1961), p. 225. We never find out if the returning Enlightened *one* sets the other prisoners free or finds it more comfortable to teach them while they are still chained up.
8. E. Grosz, *Volatile Bodies: Toward a Corporeal Feminism* (St Leonards: Allen & Unwin, 1994).
9. This relates to Nietzsche's descent and ascent relation.
10. M. Heidegger, *Being and Time*, trans. John Macquarrie and Edward Robinson (San Francisco: Harper, 1962). Heidegger, *The Question Concerning Technology and Other Essays*, trans. William Lovitt (New York: Garland Publishing, 1977). See 'The Turning', pp. 36–49. Derrida, *Of Spirit: Heidegger and the Question,* trans. Geoffrey Bennington and Rachel Bowlby (Chicago: The University of Chicago Press, 1989).

11. G. Deleuze, *Difference and Repetition*, trans. Paul Patton (New York: Columbia University Press, 1994).

12. Derrida, *Aporias*, trans. Thomas Dutoit (Stanford: Stanford University Press, 1993). Foucault, op. cit., *Death and the Labyrinth*. Foucault, op. cit., *Language, Counter-Memory, Practice*, 'A Preface to Transgression'. Foucault, op. cit., *The Foucault Reader*.

13. Deleuze and Guattari, op. cit., *A Thousand Plateaus: Capitalism and Schizophrenia*.

14. Ibid., '10,000 BC: The Geleology of Morals (Who Does the Earth Think It Is?) Stratoanalysis'.

15. Hegel, op. cit., *The Phenomenology of Spirit*. See also Barker, op. cit., *Michel Foucault: Subversions of the Subject*, pp. 178–88.

16. Heidegger, *Identity and Difference*, trans. Joan Stambaugh (New York: Harper & Row, 1969), 'Identity and Difference', p. 24.

17. Ibid.

18. See Barker, op. cit., *Michel Foucault: Subversions of the Subject*, Chapter 4, 'Drawing the subject', pp. 149–57 for an account of this by analysing *Erec and Enide* and *Yvain* by Chrétien de Troyes.

19. Heidegger, op. cit., *The Question Concerning Technology*, 'The Age of the World Picture', pp. 115–54. As an aside here, one could say something about this as providing the underpinning of the subject that colonises through the subjection of the other as the same. This also suggests the present impossibility of post-colonialism in our epoch.

20. It is a bit like reducing stock on the stove. The longer it goes on, the more it is reduced to itself.

21. Daphne du Maurier, *Rebecca* (Harmondsworth: Penguin Books, 1964), p. 5.

22. Ibid., pp. 151–2.

23. How particular interpretations of this endless possibility become 'fixed' and authenticated takes us back to Foucault's account of the Politics of Discourse; see Chapters 1 and 4.

24. This involves a double return: that of the writer to the text as well as eventually that of the reader.

25. This may have a relation to Foucault's concept of a 'non-place'. For more on what Foucault terms 'non-place' (following Nietzsche), see Foucault, op. cit., *Language, Counter-Memory, Practice*, 'Nietzsche, Genealogy, History', p. 150.

26. This ocularcentrism remains a difficulty in Heidegger.

27. Not everyone may experience this in the same way – or at all – I am thinking here of the sensation that your skin is not your 'own'. In this situation, it seems as if the surface of the skin slips away not exactly from the body of self to the body of the other but rather towards a space between where each simultaneously experiences a folding of the surfaces of the body as a *between other*.

28. Indeed, perhaps here we find some faltering elements of a critique of the relation between identity, difference and the return and their overwhelming by coming back.

29. Daphne du Maurier, *My Cousin Rachel* (Harmondsworth: Penguin Books, 1966), pp. 5 and 302.

30. Deleuze, op. cit., *Difference and Repetition*: 'Nietzsche correctly points out that if it were the One which returned, it would have begun by being unable to leave itself; if it were supposed to determine the many to resemble it, it would have begun by not losing its identity in that degradation of the similar', p. 126.

31. This raises the issue of a history of 'the philosophy of capture' and invokes the work of Deleuze and Guattari. For more on Descartes' autobiographical style, see Barker, op. cit., *Michel Foucault: Subversions of the Subject*, pp. 160–72.

32. This follows Heidegger's reversal of the Cartesian maxim.

33. Heidegger, op. cit., *Being and Time*: 'Only that entity which is "between" birth and death presents the whole which we have been seeking . . . Not only has Being-towards-the-beginning remained unnoticed; but so too, and above all, has the way in which Dasein *stretches along between* birth and death. The "connectedness of life", in which Dasein somehow maintains itself constantly, is precisely what we have overlooked in our analysis of Being-a-whole', p. 425.

34. Derrida, op. cit., *Aporias*.

35. Burchell et al., op. cit., *The Foucault Effect*, 'The Politics of Discourse', p. 71.

APPENDIX: BIOGRAPHY IN BRIEF

Listed below are some of Foucault's more significant monographs with their full French reference and the name by which they are commonly known in English. I have also included major English collections of articles and interviews. For indispensable information on Foucault's publishing career, refer to Bernauer and Rasmussen, *The Final Foucault*. Full reference details for all works in English cited below are given in the Bibliography.

1926	15 October: Michel Foucault is born in Poitiers.
1945	At the Lycée Henri IV in Paris.
1946	At the École normale supérieure.
1948	Licence de philosophie.
1949	Licence de psychologie.
1951	Agrégation de philosophie.
1952	Diplôme de psycho-pathologie from the Institute de psychologie of Paris. Assistant in the Faculty of Letters at the University of Lille.
1954	Introduction to Ludwig Binswanger, *Le rêve et l'existence*, translated as Foucault and Binswanger, *Dream and Existence*, trans. Forrest Williams and Jacob Needleman, *Review of Existential Psychology and Psychiatry*, 19:1 (1986).
1955–8	In Sweden. Assistant at the University of Uppsala.
1958	In Poland. Director of the French Centre at the University of Warsaw.
1959	Director of the French Institute in Hamburg.
1960	Maître de conférences in psychology in the Faculty of Letters at the University of Clermont-Ferrand.
1961	Thèse de doctorat ès lettres: *Folie et déraison. Histoire de la folie à l'âge classique*. Translated into English in an abridged version as *Madness and Civilisation*.
1962	Professor of Philosophy at the University of Clermont-Ferrand.

1963   *Naissance de la clinique. Une archéologie du regard médical,*
         revised in 1972. Translated into English as *The Birth of
         the Clinic: An Archaeology of Medical Perception. Raymond
         Roussel* (Paris: Gallimard, 1963). Translated as *Death and
         the Labyrinth: The World of Raymond Roussel.*
1965   Lecturing in Brazil.
1966–7   In Tunisia. *Les mots et les choses* (Paris: Gallimard, 1966).
         Translated as *The Order of Things: An Archaeology of the
         Human Sciences.*
1968   Takes part in the establishing of the University of
         Vincennes. Head of the Philosophy Department.
1969   Elected to the Collège de France. Names his Chair the
         'History of Systems of Thought'. *L'archéologie du savoir*
         (Paris: Gallimard, 1969). Translated as *The Archaeology of
         Knowledge.*
1970   2 December: his inaugural lecture at the Collège, *L'ordre
         du discours.* Translated as *Discourse on Language,* first
         appeared in English as an Appendix to the American
         edition of *The Archaeology of Knowledge.* Lectures in
         America and visits Japan.
1971   Involved in the creation of Groupe information sur les
         prisons.
1972   Visits Attica prison in the USA.
1973   Examines the birth of the prison. *Moi, Pierre Rivière,
         ayant égorgé ma mère, ma sœur et mon frère* (Paris:
         Gallimard, 1973). Translated as *I, Pierre Rivière, having
         slaughtered my mother, my sister and my brother.*
1974   Returns to teach on madness and confinement.
1975   Studies the constitution of the normal. *Surveiller et punir:
         Naissance de la prison* (Paris: Gallimard, 1975). Translated
         as *Discipline and Punish: The Birth of the Prison.*
1976   *Histoire de la sexualité 1: La volonté de savoir* (Paris:
         Gallimard, 1976). Translated as *The History of Sexuality,
         Volume 1: An Introduction.*
1977   Collected articles in *Language, Counter-Memory, Practice,*
         ed. D. Bouchard.
1978   Reports on the Iranian Revolution. Visits Japan.
         Herculine Barbin dite Alexian B. (Paris: Gallimard, 1978).
         Translated as *Herculine Barbin, Being the Recently
         Discovered Memoirs of a Nineteenth Century French
         Hermaphrodite.*
1979   Bio-politics.
1980   The Christian experience of sexuality. Collected articles
         in *Power/Knowledge,* ed. Colin Gordon.
1981   Truth and subjectivity in Greek culture.

1982   Hermeneutics of the self in ancient Greek and Roman
          practices.
1983   Truth-telling.
1984   The practice of truth-telling as a moral virtue. *Histoire de
          la sexualité 2: L'usage des plaisirs* (Paris: Gallimard, 1984).
          Translated as *The Use of Pleasure. Histoire de la sexualité 3:
          Le souci de soi* (Paris: Gallimard, 1984). Translated as *The
          Care of the Self.* Collected articles in *The Foucault Reader*,
          ed. Paul Rabinow.
1984   25 June: Foucault dies in Paris.

Major collections published after the death of Foucault:

Collected articles in *Politics Philosophy Culture Interviews and Other
     Writings 1977–1984*, ed. Lawrence Kritzman.
Collected articles in *Remarks on Marx*, trans. R. James Goldstein
     and James Cascaito.
Collected articles in *Foucault Live: Collected Interviews, 1961–1984*,
     ed. Sylvère Lotringer.

Important collections of essays on the work of Foucault are:

Armstrong, T. J. (trans.), *Michel Foucault Philosopher*.
Bernauer, J. and D. Rasmussen (eds), *The Final Foucault*.
Burchell, G., C. Gordon and P. Miller, *The Foucault Effect: Studies
     in Governmentality*.
Diamond, I. and L. Quinby (eds), *Feminism and Foucault:
     Reflections on Resistance*.
Gutting, Gary (ed.), *The Cambridge Companion to Foucault*.
Hoy, David Couzens (ed.), *Foucault: A Critical Reader*.

For general biographical information, refer to D. Eribon, *Michel
     Foucault* (trans. Betsy Wing), and D. Macey, *The Lives of Michel
     Foucault*.

For more information on the work of Michel Foucault, contact:

Bibliothèque du Saulchoir,
Association pour le Centre Michel Foucault,
43 *bis*, rue de la Glacière,
F-75013 Paris,
France.

BIBLIOGRAPHY

Althusser, L., *Lenin and Other Essays* (London: New Left Books, 1977).

Barker, P., *Michel Foucault: Subversions of the Subject* (Hemel Hempstead: Harvester Wheatsheaf, 1994).

Barker, P., 'Foucault's Sublime: E-mail to Postumius Terentianus', in Claire O'Farrell (ed.), *Foucault: The Legacy* (Brisbane: Queensland University of Technology, 1997).

Burchell, G., C. Gordon and P. Miller, *The Foucault Effect: Studies in Governmentality* (Hemel Hempstead: Harvester Wheatsheaf, 1991).

Burke, E., *A Philosophical Enquiry into the Origin of our Ideas of the Sublime and Beautiful*, ed. J. T. Boulton (London: Routledge and Kegan Paul, 1958).

de Sade, Marquis Justine, *Philosophy in the Bedroom and Other Writings* (New York: Grove Press, 1965).

Deleuze, G., *Foucault*, trans. Seán Hand (Minneapolis: University of Minnesota Press, 1990).

Deleuze, G., *Difference and Repetition*, trans. Paul Patton (New York: Columbia University Press, 1994).

Deleuze, G. and F. Guattari, *A Thousand Plateaus: Capitalism and Schizophrenia*, trans. B. Massumi (Minneapolis: University of Minnesota Press, 1987).

Derrida, J., *Writing and Difference*, trans. Alan Bass (Chicago: The University of Chicago Press, 1978).

Derrida, J., *Of Spirit: Heidegger and the Question*, trans. Geoffrey Bennington and Rachel Bowlby (Chicago: The University of Chicago Press, 1989).

Derrida, J., *Aporias*, trans. Thomas Dutoit (Stanford: Stanford University Press, 1993).

Descartes, R., *The Philosophical Works of Descartes, vols I & II*, trans. Elizabeth Haldane and G. R. T. Ross (London: Cambridge University Press, 1967).

Dreyfus, Hubert L. and Paul Rabinow, *Michel Foucault: Beyond Structuralism and Hermeneutics* (Brighton: The Harvester Press, 1982).

du Maurier, D., *Rebecca* (Harmondsworth: Penguin Books, 1964).

du Maurier, D., *My Cousin Rachel* (Harmondsworth: Penguin Books, 1966).

Elders, Fons, *Reflexive Water: The Basic Concerns of Mankind* (London: Souvenir Press, 1974).

Foss, P. and P. Taylor (eds), *Art and Text, Burnout*, 16 (1984/5), M. Foucault, 'Interview: The Regard for Truth'.

Foucault, M., *The Discourse on Language*, appendix to *The Archaeology of Knowledge*, trans. A. M. Sheridan Smith (New York: Pantheon Books, 1972).

Foucault, M., *The Archaeology of Knowledge*, trans. A. M. Sheridan Smith (London: Tavistock, 1972).

Foucault, M., *The Birth of the Clinic: An Archaeology of Medical Perception*, trans. A. M. Sheridan (London: Tavistock, 1976).

Foucault, M., *Language, Counter-Memory, Practice: Selected Essays and Interviews*, ed. D. Bouchard (New York: Cornell University Press, 1977).

Foucault, M., *I, Pierre Rivière: having slaughtered my mother, my sister and my brother . . .* (Harmondsworth, Penguin Books, 1978).

Foucault, M., *Madness and Civilisation*, trans. Richard Howard (London: Tavistock, 1979).

Foucault, M., *The History of Sexuality, Volume 1: An Introduction*, trans. Robert Hurley (London: Allen Lane, 1979).

Foucault, M., *Discipline and Punish: The Birth of the Prison*, trans. Alan Sheridan (Harmondsworth: Penguin Books, 1979).

Foucault, M., *Power/Knowledge*, ed. Colin Gordon (New York: Pantheon Books, 1980).

Foucault, M., *The Order of Things: An Archaeology of the Human Sciences* (London: Tavistock, 1980).

Foucault, M., *Herculine Barbin, Being the Recently Discovered Memoirs of a Nineteenth Century French Hermaphrodite*, trans. Richard McDougall (New York: Pantheon Books, 1980).

Foucault, M., *The Foucault Reader*, ed. Paul Rabinow (New York: Pantheon Books, 1984).

Foucault, M., *Death and the Labyrinth: The World of Raymond Roussel*, trans. Charles Ruas (New York: Doubleday, 1986).

Foucault, M., *Technologies of the Self*, ed. L. H. Martin, H. Gutman and P. H. Hutton (London: Tavistock Publications; The University of Massachusetts Press, 1988).

Foucault, M., *Politics Philosophy Culture Interviews and Other Writings 1977–1984*, ed. Lawrence Kritzman (New York: Routledge, 1990).

Foucault, M., *Remarks on Marx*, trans. R. James Goldstein and James Cascaito (New York: Semiotext(e), Columbia University, 1991).

Foucault, M., *Foucault Live: Collected Interviews, 1961–1984*, ed. Sylvère Lotringer (New York: Semiotext(e), Columbia University, 1996).

Foucault, M. and M. Blanchot, *Foucault/Blanchot* (New York: Zone Books, 1987).

Grosz, E., *Volatile Bodies: Toward a Corporeal Feminism* (St Leonards: Allen & Unwin, 1994).

Hegel, G. W. F., *The Phenomenology of Spirit*, trans. A. V. Miller (London: Oxford University Press, 1979).

Heidegger, M., *Being and Time*, trans. John Macquarrie and Edward Robinson (San Francisco: Harper, 1962).

Heidegger, M., *Identity and Difference*, trans. Joan Stambaugh (New York: Harper & Row, 1969).

Heidegger, M., *The Question Concerning Technology and Other Essays*, trans. William Lovitt (New York: Garland Publishing, 1977).

Heidegger, M., *Basic Writings*, ed. David Farrell Krell (London: Routledge, 1993).

Kant, I., *Observations on the Feeling of the Beautiful and the Sublime*, trans. John T. Goldthwait (Berkeley: University of California Press, 1991).

Librett, Jeffrey S. (trans.), *Of the Sublime: Presence in Question* (New York: State University of New York Press, 1993).

Longinus, *Longinus on Elevation of Style*, trans. T. G. Tucker (Melbourne: Melbourne University Press, 1935).

Merquior, J. G., *Foucault* (London: Fontana Press/Collins, 1985).

Miller, J., *The Passion of Michel Foucault* (New York: Simon and Schuster, 1993).

Morris, M. and P. Patton (eds), *Michel Foucault: Power, Truth, Strategy* (Sydney: Feral, 1979).

Nietzsche, F., *Daybreak – Thoughts on the Prejudices of Morality*, trans. R. J. Hollingdale (Cambridge: Cambridge University Press, 1983).

Plato, *The Republic of Plato*, trans. F. M. Cornford (Oxford: Clarendon Press, 1961).

OTHER SOURCES CONSULTED

Arac, J. (ed.), *After Foucault: Humanistic Knowledge, Postmodern Challenges* (New Brunswick: Rutgers University Press, 1991).

Armstrong, T. J. (trans.), *Michel Foucault Philosopher* (Hemel Hempstead: Harvester Wheatsheaf, 1992).

Ball, S. J. (ed.), *Foucault and Education: Disciplines and Knowledge* (London: Routledge, 1990).

Bernauer, J. and D. Rasmussen (eds), *The Final Foucault* (Cambridge, MA: The MIT Press, 1988).

Cousins, M. and A. Hussain, *Michel Foucault* (London: Macmillan, 1984).

Diamond, I. and L. Quinby (eds), *Feminism and Foucault: Reflections on Resistance* (Boston, MA: Northeastern University Press, 1988).

Eribon, D., *Michel Foucault*, trans. Betsy Wing (Cambridge, MA: Harvard University Press, 1992).

Foucault, M., *Mental Illness and Psychology*, trans. Alan Sheridan (New York: Harper & Row, 1976).

Foucault, M., *This is Not a Pipe* (Berkeley: University of California Press, 1983).

Foucault, M., *The Use of Pleasure, The History of Sexuality, Volume 2*, trans. Robert Hurley (New York: Pantheon Books, 1985).

Foucault, M., *The Care of the Self, The History of Sexuality, Volume 3*, trans. Robert Hurley (New York: Pantheon Books, 1986).

Foucault, M. and L. Binswanger, *Dream and Existence*, trans. Forrest Williams and Jacob Needleman, *Review of Existential Psychology and Psychiatry*, 19:1 (1986).

Gane, M. (ed.), *Towards a Critique of Foucault* (London: Routledge and Kegan Paul, 1986).

Gane, M. and T. Johnson (eds), *Foucault's New Domains* (London: Routledge, 1993).

Gutting, Gary (ed.), *The Cambridge Companion to Foucault* (Cambridge: Cambridge University Press, 1994).

Halperin, David M., *Saint Foucault: Towards a Gay Hagiography* (Oxford: Oxford University Press, 1995).

Hoy, David Couzens (ed.), *Foucault: A Critical Reader* (Oxford: Basil Blackwell, 1986).

Lemert, Charles C. and G. Gillan, *Michel Foucault: Social Theory as Transgression* (New York: Columbia University Press, 1982).

Macey, D., *The Lives of Michel Foucault* (London: Vintage, 1994).

McHoul, A. and W. Grace, *A Foucault Primer: Discourse, Power and the Subject* (Carlton: Melbourne University Press, 1993).

Major-Poetzl, P., *Michel Foucault's Archaeology of Western Culture: Towards a New Science of History* (Chapel Hill: The University of North Carolina Press, 1983).

Minson, J., *Genealogies of Morals* (London: Macmillan, 1985).

Poster, M., 'Foucault and critical theory: the uses of discourse analysis', *Humanities in Society*, 5:3–4 (Summer and Fall 1982), University of Southern California, 1983.

Ramazanoglu, C. (ed.), *Up Against Foucault: Explorations of Some Tensions Between Foucault and Feminism* (London: Routledge, 1993).

Sawicki, J., *Disciplining Foucault: Feminism, Power, and the Body* (New York: Routledge, 1991).

Sheridan, A., *Michel Foucault: The Will to Truth* (London: Tavistock, 1980).

Smart, B., *Michel Foucault* (Chichester: Ellis Horwood, 1985).

INDEX